The Asbury Theologica
Christian Revitali.

M000318291

This volume is published in collaboration with the Center for the Study of World Christian Revitalization Movements, a cooperative initiative of Asbury Theological Seminary faculty. Building on the work of the previous Wesleyan/Holiness Studies Center at the Seminary, the Center provides a focus for research in the Wesleyan Holiness and other related Christian renewal movements, including Pietism and Pentecostal movements, which have had a world impact. The research seeks to develop analytical models of these movements, including their biblical and theological assessment. Using an interdisciplinary approach, the Center bridges relevant discourses in several areas in order to gain insights for effective Christian mission globally. It recognizes the need for conducting research that combines insights from the history of evangelical renewal and revival movements with anthropological and religious studies literature on revitalization movements. It also networks with similar or related research and study centers around the world, in addition to sponsoring its own research projects.

A key feature in revitalization literature is the exploration of the distinctive ecclesiology that gathers humanity across racial as well as ethnic and cultural barriers. This study of sanctified unity ecclesiology in early holiness Pentecostalism addresses this aspect in an important study bringing empathy to what it means to live holiness from a counter cultural context, on the "other" side of the color line. Thomas grounds his study in the historical and theological framework of the radical holiness movement that pioneered in breaking down this racial barrier to Christian unity. He contends for the importance of a recovery of the doctrine of entire sanctification, joined to African American folk theology, as being the determinative factors in promoting racial inclusion within the Wesleyan holiness wing of early Pentecostalism. In giving focus to this theme, Thomas offers an important contribution to the ongoing research of the Revitalization Center, and to the Pentecostal and Charismatic Studies Series in Christian Revitalization Movements, in particular.

J. Steven O'Malley
General Editor
The Asbury Theological Seminary Studies in Christian Revitalization

Sub-Series Foreword
Pentecostal and Charismatic Studies

Of all the renewal traditions that have engaged the theological landscape, the Pentecostal Movement has undoubtedly made the most significant impact since it emerged at the turn of the twentieth century. Starting as a revival in a small African-American congregation on Azusa Street in Los Angeles, California, the movement soon swept the world, establishing itself in more than forty countries in the first three years. One hundred years later Pentecostalism has grown to an estimated 500 million global adherents or approximately twenty-five percent of all of Christendom. In the same manner that Wesleyanism burst beyond the bounds of Methodism to embrace an interdenominational holiness movement following the American Civil War in the nineteenth century, Pentecostalism transcended denominational lines in the form of the Charismatic Movement during the second half of the twentieth century.

This sub-series is designed to explore the historical, theological and intercultural dimensions of these twin twentieth-century restorationists' traditions from a global perspective. In recent years several scholars have argued that in addition to spirit-baptism evidenced by speaking in tongues, a second unique development of Pentecostalism, was that that William Seymour in seeing the Azusa Street Revival as the restoration of Pentecost meant that for the first time since the first century all nations and races were being brought back together and were to be fully integrated in local assemblies. In this volume, Joe Thomas breaks new ground showing that this insight had been significantly developed and implemented in the radical holiness movement which emerged in the 1880's, led by Daniel Warner and the Evening Light Saints (Church of God, Anderson), along with such groups as Martin Wells Knapp and the International Holiness Union and Prayer League, Edwin Harvey and the Burning Bush (Metropolitan Church Association) and James Washburn and the California Holiness Association. Looking collectively at these and other radical holiness groups, Thomas has added a significant piece of the historical puzzle as to how Pentecostalism evolved from the Wesleyan tradition.

D. William Faupel

Perfect Harmony

Interracial Churches in Early Holiness-Pentecostalism, 1880-1909

Joseph L. Thomas

Asbury Theological Seminary Series:
The Study of World Christian Revitalization Movements in
Pentecostal/Charismatic Studies

EMETH PRESS
www.emethpress.com

Perfect Harmony: Interracial Churches in Early Holiness-Pentecostalism, 1880-1909

Copyright © 2014 Joseph L. Thomas

Printed in the United States of America on acid-free paper. All rights reserved. No part of this book may be reproduced, or stored in a retrieval system or transmitted in any form or by any means, electronic, mechanical, photocopying, recording, scanning or otherwise, except as permitted by the 1976 United States Copyright Act, or with the prior written permission of Emeth Press. Requests for permission should be addressed to: Emeth Press, P. O. Box 23961, Lexington, KY 40523-3961. http://www.emethpress.com.

Library of Congress Cataloging-in-Publication Data

Thomas, Joseph L.
 Perfect Harmony: Interracial Churches in Early Holiness-Pentecostalism, 1880-1909 / Joseph L. Thomas.
    pages cm. -- (The Asbury Theological Seminary series in Christian revitalization movements in Pentecostal/charismatic studies)
 Includes index.
 ISBN 978-1-60947-078-4 (alk. paper)
1. Holiness churches--Doctrines--History--19th century. 2. Pentecostal churches--Doctrines--History--19th century. 3. Holiness churches--Doctrines--History--20th century. 4. Pentecostal churches--Doctrines--History--20th century. 5. Church. 6. Race relations--Religious aspects--Christianity. 7. Ethnic relations--Religious aspects--Christianity. 8. Reconciliation--Religious aspects--Christianity. I. Title.
 BX7990.H6T46 2014
 230'.994--dc23
                    2014011947

"This is a queer camp. I sometimes look on with amazement. Five distinct races or nationalities, three generations (and some between), diversities of make-up, religious training, temperament, etc., yet God enables us to keep in *perfect harmony, without an effort to do so.* Only God could do it. Hallelujah?"

Laura Goings (*Pentecost,* 1896)

To Audra, Cristabel, and Mae

May my work equal your sacrifice

Contents

Foreword

Perfect Harmony joins the theological chorus of voices proclaiming theologies of racial equality. As a work of historical theology, *Perfect Harmony* exposes the readers to theological voices of the late nineteenth century and early twentieth century that expressed in fragmented and, occasionally, lucid ways a vision of church as a community of racial unity.

Perfect Harmony uncovers an ecclesiology affirming racial diversity that found grounding in the doctrine of sanctification which generated the interracial and multiethnic ecclesial practices which emerged in the radical holiness movement and early Pentecostalism. In this book, Joseph Thomas provides a theological analysis to frame interracial and multiethnic Christian fellowship as an expression of what he named "sanctified unity" marked by "perfect love."

Perfect Harmony introduces the reader to a fine work of historical theology. Thomas explores how the doctrine of holiness becomes blended with the doctrine of Christian unity to craft an ecclesiology of sanctified unity which sought to overcome denominational and racial divisions and restore the unity among Christians that marked the New Testament Church. Consequently, restorationism with its quest to recover apostolic Christianity drives the theological project that Thomas probes. Additionally, Thomas adeptly demonstrates how a theology of the atonement, sanctification, Christian unity, and racial unity laced with eschatological expectation and restorationist proclivities provided the intellectual architecture to construct an interracial ecclesiology of sanctified unity.

In *Perfect Harmony*, Thomas retraces the Scriptural bases to the ecclesiology of sanctified unity. In overcoming racial disunity, he illustrates how particular white and African American holiness leaders offered an exegesis of Galatians 3:28 which proposed a parallelism between Jews and Gentiles and contemporary whites and Blacks. As well, Thomas notes how early holiness leaders led their followers to see that just as Scripture demanded an end to the divisions between Jew and Gentile it likewise demanded an end to the racial divisions of their own time. The history of biblical interpretation finds expression in the kind of historical theology that Thomas promotes.

The climax of Thomas's historical theology of sanctified unity is the theology of Azusa Street Revival. Thomas persuasively demonstrates how the radical holiness view of Christian unity fueled the theological and ecclesial quest for an interracial and multiethnic fellowship in Los Angeles. The Azusa Street Revival brought together various theological streams from the radical holiness movement that proclaimed an ecclesiology of sanctified unity.

Perfect Harmony complements the historical theology probed with an historical reconstruction of the interracial and multiethnic experiments that practiced sanctified unity by the radical holiness people and early Pentecostals. Thomas identifies interracial ecclesiology to be key to the bi-racial or interracial ministries of holiness leaders such as Daniel S. Warner, Martin Wells Knapp, J. F. Washburn, Laura Goings and George Goings as well as Pentecostal pioneers such as William J. Seymour, Glenn Cook, Charles Harrison Mason, Mack Pinson and Leonard P. Adams. He presents the revivals and camp meetings in which these and other leaders practiced sanctified unity within racial mixed audience.

Historiographically, Thomas contends that the doctrine of sanctification undergirded the interracial and multiethnic ecclesiology that countered the segregationist ecclesiologies of that era. His position challenges the scholarship that highlights the Pentecostal Baptism of the Holy Spirit and the doctrine of initial evidence as sole theological basis of early Pentecostal interracial and multiethnic ecclesiology. To him, the ecclesiology of sanctified unity is foundational to early Pentecostal theological formation.

Perfect Harmony strikes a theological chord that sounds out an ecclesial trajectory that ran along the margins of American Protestantism over a century ago. Yet, this theological chord resonates with the call for a theology of Christian unity that can foster racial unity and equality. *Perfect Harmony* graciously and thoughtfully invites the reader to hear an earlier theological composition of this ecclesial vision.

Dr. David D. Daniels
Henry Winters Luce Professor of World Christianity
McCormick Theological Seminary
Chicago, Illinois

Acknowledgments

I cannot begin to thank everyone who was instrumental in helping me complete *Perfect Harmony: Interracial Churches in Early Holiness-Pentecostalism, 1880-1909*. An inspirational conversation here, an encouraging word there, multiplied dozens of times over the years, makes it necessary for me to offer a general "thank you" to a host of friends, colleagues and mentors. Having said that, there are still some individuals without whom this book would not have happened. To them I wish to provide special recognition.

The encouragement and support of Urbana Theological Seminary made it possible for me to complete the writing of this book. Dr. Ken Cuffey, Dr. Todd Daly, Dr. Mike McQueen, and Dr. Peter Spychalla have been outstanding colleagues and discussion partners through this process.

I am especially indebted to Church Historian Dr. Douglas Sweeney from Trinity Evangelical Divinity School. His example of a Christian scholar stays with me each and every day. More than a mentor, I consider Doug to be a confidant and friend.

I also want to thank Dr. David Daniels from McCormick Theological Seminary in Chicago for his discerning eye. In the midst of his very full schedule David made room for countless hours of conversation on the strengths and weaknesses of my research and thinking. His expertise in the field of black holiness-pentecostalism has strengthened my research and any faults that remain are my own.

Finally, I want to say a special thank you to Dr. Amos Yong and Dr. W. David Faupel. Dr. Yong offered me crucial encouragement along the path to publication and introduced me to Emeth Press. Dr. Faupel was my editor at Emeth Press and provided especially helpful suggestions as to how to strengthen *Perfect Harmony*.

Historical scholarship cannot be done without the existence of archives and the archivists who operate them. I deeply thank the generosity and help from Wayne Warner, Glen Gohr, and Joyce Lee of the Flower Heritage Pentecostal Center in Springfield, Missouri. Their encouragement and enthusiasm at the outset of this study provided a momentum that helped carry me through the long hours of looking through countless reels of microfilm. I also want to thank Doug Welch and his staff at the Church of God archives at Anderson University in Anderson, Indiana. His willingness to sit down and talk through my project when it was at its inception helped to clarify my direction of research. And finally, I wish to thank the staff at Asbury Theological Seminary for allowing me the use of their fine collection at Wilmore, Kentucky.

Lastly, I want to thank my wife, Dr. Audra Marie Thomas, for the emotional, spiritual and financial support that made this work possible. She is a great team player, and with the help of God brings to life the biblical saying that "three cords are not easily broken."

Introduction

The Development of Sanctified Unity: Ecclesiology in Early Holiness-Pentecostalism

Historians of the Holiness and Pentecostal traditions have documented the counter-cultural social dynamics that existed in many holiness-pentecostal churches at the end of the nineteenth and the beginning of the twentieth century. Within these churches the coming together of different ethnicities in fellowship and worship was one of the outstanding features that developed. That Jim Crow legislation and attitudes guided the social habits of most Americans during this time makes the existence of interracial churches particularly unique. As historians of the two traditions have worked to determine the exact causes for such counter-cultural behavior each has come to emphasize a different interpretation. Not surprisingly, historians of the radical Holiness movement have placed their stress on the ecclesiological unity that undergirded the preaching and theological reflection of the saints.[1] Known as "come-outers" before 1894 and "put-outers" afterwards, they leveled harsh criticism at the denominational churches and called for the restoration of the biblical "Church of God."[2] Advocates of radical holiness believed that denominationalism at its root originated in the selfish nature of man and must *ipso facto* keep the church divided. Their

---

1. "The Church of God reformation's message of unity of all believers . . . made a very strong interracial position inherent to the message itself." See John W. V. Smith, *The Quest for Holiness and Unity* (Anderson, Ind: Warner Press, Inc., 1980), and Rodney Layne Reed, "Toward the Integrity of Social Ethics and Personal Ethics in the Holiness Movement, 1880-1910" (Ph.D. diss., Drew University, 1995).

2. The Methodist Episcopal Church, South made its pivotal decision in 1894 to deny holiness evangelists the privilege to travel the Methodist parish circuit. This was followed in 1898 with another ruling that gave the parish minister the right to refuse the entry of any holiness evangelist to their parish. The net effect was the ouster of the Holiness movement from the Methodist Episcopal churches.

call for the reconstituting of the Church of God meant for them, in contrast, the restoration of the unity of the body of Christ.

Historians of the Pentecostal movement, likewise, have staked their arguments on what was *sui generis* at the Azusa Street revival. Most interpretations proffer that the practice of multiethnic fellowship at the Apostolic Faith Mission was rooted in the doctrine of Spirit baptism. The first pentecostals believed, it is argued, that the eschatological outpouring of the Spirit in Los Angeles broke down the wall of partition between men and women, white and black, and rich and poor.

So far as they go neither one of these historical evaluations is incorrect. But each leaves out the critical factor that advocates of radical holiness at the end of the nineteenth century and the leadership of the Azusa Street revival both indicated was decisive in establishing an ethnically unified church: the experience of the "second blessing." This work, then, will close the gap in the scholarship and demonstrate that entire sanctification, as part of a larger ecclesiological paradigm which I have termed "sanctified unity," was the primary cause for racial inclusion in the Wesleyan wing of the early Holiness-Pentecostal movement. I will also note the assistance that African-American folk theology contributed to the meeting of the races in Holiness-Pentecostal churches. But as has been noted by contemporaries of the time and by later historians, the problem of racial segregation was a problem caused by whites, not blacks. After the Civil War, through the Reconstruction years and during the rise of Jim Crow legislation, most African Americans desired to integrate into American society. The truth of the matter is that it was mainly whites who needed a means, a catalyst, to help them overcome their historic prejudice against non-Caucasians. Within the radical Holiness movement, the writings of those whites who did cross the cultural barrier of race and ethnicity indicate that the experience of entire sanctification provided the medium for new ecclesiological possibilities in their church lives.

Holiness Historical Perspectives

It is no surprise that the most sustained reflection on the issue of interracial and multiethnic fellowship in the radical Holiness movement comes from historians associated with the Church of God (Anderson). The denomination has developed an excellent educational infrastructure with its flagship school Anderson University, located at the denominational headquarters in Indiana. And even though the church's present state of fellowship is essentially segregated, it still has taken seriously its interracial past.

Church of God historians always have considered ecclesiology to be critical to the church's self-identity. Since the church came into existence out of period of deep ecclesiological reflection this is not surprising. Daniel S. Warner, the founder of the Church of God Reformation Movement, had a mystical vision in 1881 where he "saw the church." Warner had been conflicted for some time over his denunciation of denominational sectarianism, which he deemed "Babylon," and his involvement with Protestant organizations. A member of various organizations that preached holiness doctrine, he never could reconcile Jesus' high priestly prayer for unity (John 17), flowing out of a sanctified life, and the division that plagued the nineteenth-century American church. After his vision he broke away from "Babylon" and began to preach a message of holiness and unity. He, and other Church of God evangelists, soon found that the church's message met with a positive response from within black and other minority communities.

Church of God denominational historians have written extensively on the theological link between the doctrines of holiness and unity. John W. V. Smith's *The Quest for Holiness and Unity* is an entire history of the denomination written from the perspective of the church's ecclesiological paradigm. Barry L. Callen, similarly, wrote *It's God's Church! The Life and Legacy of Daniel Sydney Warner*, demonstrating that Warner repudiated on biblical grounds that membership in God's church was based on "formal sect recognition."[3] More recently, Merle Strege, in *I Saw the Church: The life of the Church of God Told Theologically*, makes it plain that the founders of the church firmly held to the belief that without holiness there could be no unity. As the earliest radical holiness group to separate from the mainline denominational system, the Church of God Reformation Movement was the first to formulate sanctified unity ecclesiology as it applied to the corporate church, that is, its institutional structure.[4]

The sanctified unity of the corporate church also affected the communal body of Christ, or the daily fellowship among believers, during the first generation of the Church of God Reformation Movement. Race, gender and social class tended to get sublimated in the throes of restoring the New Testament church. Strege concludes that the early adherents tended to read Gal 3:28 literally.[5] Cheryl J. Sanders, Church of God historian and ethicist, notes, as well, that the strong belief in the transforming power of entire sanctification created a transgressive space[6] for marginalized peoples to participate in egalitarian worship.[7] Finally, Callen states the ecclesiological paradigm of sanctified unity, corporately and communally:

> The "perfect love" of sanctification, it was argued, enables Christians to live above sin, including the sin of rending the body of Christ. Human lines of

---

3. Callen, *It's God's Church*, 93.

4. See Merle D. Strege, *I Saw the Church: The life of the Church of God Told Theologically* (Anderson, IN: Warner Press, 2002).

5. Ibid., 147.

6. A transgressive space is a place where the social mores of a society can be violated. In the case of the radical Holiness movement the fellowshipping and worshiping of black, brown and white saints together turned their churches, revivals, tent meetings and conferences into transgressive spaces.

7. Cheryl J. Sanders, *Saints in Exile: The Holiness-Pentecostal Experience in African American Religion and Culture* (New York: Oxford University Press, 1996), 32, 134.

denomination, race, sex, and social status are to be discounted, even ignored in the face of the transforming grace of God in Christ.[8]

While these historians have captured well the radical holiness ecclesiology that transformed the Church of God Reformation Movement into a counter-culture movement, their denominational focus has kept them from addressing the implications of sanctified unity ecclesiology across the nationwide radical Holiness movement. Only recently have Church of God historians begun to recognize the important connections between their church and William J. Seymour, leader of the highly interracial and multiethnic Azusa Street revival.[9] As I will argue in chapter five, Seymour's radical holiness roots were more important to his interracial ecclesiology than the effects of the doctrine of Spirit baptism. Furthermore, an in depth analysis of the interplay between sanctified unity ecclesiology and racial and ethnic inclusion is missing in Holiness historiography. This monograph, then, will demonstrate that the sanctified unity ecclesiology initiated in the Church of God Reformation Movement contributed to and was a part of a larger movement of radical holiness folk who sought to do away with worldly divisions within the body of Christ. Although prejudicial patterns existed in many social arrangements within the late nineteenth and early twentieth-century American church, this dissertation will focus narrowly on the overcoming of ethnic segregationism as practiced in radical holiness-pentecostal churches. It will then demonstrate the influence of sanctified unity ecclesiology on the multiethnic revival at Azusa Street.

Pentecostal Historical Perspectives

The first written accounts detailing the extraordinary events that took place at the Apostolic Faith Mission in Los Angeles, between 1906 and 1909, claimed that the revival was initiated and led by the Holy Spirit. Neither human leader nor historical context was recognized as instrumental in the eschatological outbreak experienced in Los Angeles. The "Golden Oldies," to use Grant Wacker's description of the first pentecostal histories[10], surmised that the final outpouring of God's "latter rain," understood as commencing at the Azusa Street revival, would sweep away all man-made institutions and human conventions and restore the church to the pristine days of Pentecost. Several decades of pentecostal scholarship have undone this original assumption revealing a rich historical background which in large

---

8. Callen, *It's God's Church*, 100.

9. Cheryl J. Sanders, *Empowerment Ethics for a Liberated People: A Path to African American Social Transformation* (Minneapolis, Minn.: Fortress Press, 1995), 74.

10. See Grant A. Wacker, "Are the Golden Oldies Still Worth Playing? Reflections on History Writing among Early Pentecostals," *Pneuma* 8 (Fall 1986): 81-100.

part shaped the events at the Azusa Street Mission.[11] It is now accepted that Pentecostalism emerged out of the radical wing of the Holiness movement. Antecedent doctrines and practices that defined radical holiness, such as healing, premillennialism, Wesleyan sanctification and the "baptism of the Holy Spirit", were all represented in the Azusa worship services.[12] Most of the revival participants were part of an already well-established network of radical holiness groups. These radical holiness groups included local church networks such as the Southern California and Arizona Holiness Association, the Metropolitan Church Association, and the Pentecostal Church of the Nazarene. From around the nation holiness radicals also flocked to Los Angeles representing, for example, the holiness-oriented Church of God in Christ and the Fire-Baptized Holiness church. Finally, comprehensive research into William J. Seymour's background confirms that his contacts in the radical Holiness movement were quite extensive. Seymour first joined the radical Holiness movement in Cincinnati, Ohio, attending Martin Wells Knapp's God's Bible School and Missionary Training Home. A short time later he became a licensed minister with the Church of God Reformation Movement. Finally, he joined Charles Parham and his Apostolic Faith Mission in Houston, Texas. All three associations place Seymour at the heart of the radical Holiness movement.[13] That so much effort has been spent demonstrating the historical and theological links between radical holiness and pentecostalism makes it all the more surprising to discover the absence of a similar connection in the historiography evaluating interracial and multiethnic interaction at Azusa. This is especially true when it comes to exploring the ecclesiological formulation of racial and ethnic unity at the Apostolic Faith Mission.

Most scholars still construe the creation of an interracial and multiethnic fellowship at Azusa, or to use Ithiel C. Clemmons' rich descriptive phrase, "a divine glossolalic community of human equality," as primarily the result of the pentecostal doctrine and experience of Spirit baptism.[14] For example, Douglas Nelson summarizes Seymour's theological approach to interracialism as formulated within the third work doctrine of Spirit baptism. "The primary work of the Holy Spirit is not to produce glossolalia but to 'make all races and nations into one common family.'"[15] His ground-breaking and

---

11. See Augustus Cerillo Jr. and Grant A. Wacker, "Bibliography and Historiography," in *The New International Dictionary of Pentecostal and Charismatic Movements,* ed. Stanley M. Burgess and Eduardo M. Van Der Maas (Grand Rapids: Zondervan, 2002), 382-405.
12. See Donald W. Dayton, *Theological Roots of Pentecostalism* (Metuchen, N.J.: Scarecrow, 1987; reprint, Peabody, Mass.: Hendrickson, 1994).
13. Douglas Nelson, "For Such a Time as This: The Story of Bishop William J. Seymour and the Azusa Street Revival" (Ph.D. diss., University of Birmingham, 1981), 162-168.
14. Ithiel C. Clemmons, "True Koinonia: Pentecostal Hopes and Historical Realities-Presidential Address," *Pneuma* 4 (Spring 1982): 51.
15. Nelson, "For Such a Time as This," 204.

influential dissertation argued that racial unity was the paramount sign of the baptism of the Holy Spirit, rather than the "initial physical evidence" of glossolalia as advocated by Classical Pentecostals.[16] Nelson postulated that Seymour's propensity to worship with radical holiness churches that practiced interracial fellowship prior to the Azusa Street revival reflected his strong desire for a truly egalitarian church community. Indeed, he is the first scholar to bring to the attention of modern Church historians the interaction of Seymour with both the Church of God Reformation Movement and Martin Wells Knapp's God's Bible School and Missionary Training Home, both vigorous advocates for breaking down ecclesiological walls between blacks and whites.[17] However, since Douglas did not explore underneath the racially inclusive surface of these communities and uncover the significance of sanctified unity ecclesiology in radical holiness theology, he was left no option but to posit in the work of Spirit baptism the development of interracial and multiethnic fellowship at Azusa Street. Specifically, he completely overlooked the importance of Wesleyan sanctification in the formation of corporate and communal unity in the ecclesiological explanations of the Azusa Street leadership.

Both Iain MacRobert and William Faupel follow Nelson's lead on this account. MacRobert's remarks directly echo Nelson's, "White Pentecostals valued and retained glossolalia but neglected or rejected the equality and unity which the Spirit brought to Azusa Street."[18] Faupel, as well, bypasses Seymour's mandatory and secondary step of Wesleyan sanctification and its connection to interracial unity when he restates Nelson's interpretation thus: "The Cross itself, he [Seymour] contended, was designed by God to draw all mankind together at their point of commonality-their sinfulness. Pentecost was a gift of enablement that came upon the newborn children of God . . . to heal 'the deepest breaches of humanity' (racism). . ."[19]

---

16. The latter position is historically held by classical Pentecostal churches that are predominantly white.

17. William Faupel establishes that Parham's Apostolic Faith movement also practiced a significant degree of interracialism, although within a paternalistic framework. See D. William Faupel, *The Everlasting Gospel: The Significance of Eschatology in the Development of Pentecostal Thought* (Sheffield, England: Sheffield Academic Press, 1996), 211.

18. Iain MacRobert, *The Black Roots and White Racism of Early Pentecostalism in the USA* (New York: St. Martin's, 1988), 88.

19. D. William Faupel, "William H. Durham and the Finished Work of Calvary," in *Pentecost, Mission and Ecumenism: Essays on Intercultural Theology*, Studies in the Intercultural History of Christianity, No. 75, ed. Jan A. B. Jongereel (Frankfurt am Main: Peter Lang, 1992), 88; Faupel, *The Everlasting Gospel*, 198. For a more popular presentation of Pentecostalism that follows Nelson's interpretation see Harvey Cox, *Fire from Heaven: The Rise of Pentecostal Spirituality and the Reshaping of Religion in the Twenty-First Century* (Reading, Mass.: Addison-Wesley, 1995), 47, 61; For a denominational history written within Nelson's paradigm see Ithiel C. Clemmons,

Douglas Jacobsen's *Thinking in the Spirit: Theologies of the Early Pentecostal Movement* is the most recent, substantial attempt to take seriously the theology of early Pentecostalism.[20] Published in 2003, it demonstrates all the marks of the dominant historiographical view. Jacobsen omits any mention of the role sanctification might have played in the ecclesiological understanding of racial and ethnic inclusion at the Apostolic Faith Mission and, instead, places all the emphasis on Spirit baptism:

> Perhaps the ultimate sign of the baptism of the Spirit—was communal rather than individual. If the real sign of the baptism of the Spirit was more love for others, the communal manifestation of that love was the ability to care for and respect each other across the lines of race, class, gender, and age that normally separated people. And that is what Seymour and others claimed happened at the Azusa revival. *The Apostolic Faith* paper reported that "all classes and nationalities meet on a common ground."[21]

Even more to the point, he demonstrates unfamiliarity with the details of radical holiness theology when he rewrites Frank Bartleman's famous phrase, substituting "Spirit" for "blood," to say, "Thus it was not without reason that many pentecostals came to believe that the color line was being washed away by the Spirit."[22] Bartleman's remark referred to the work of sanctification, not Spirit baptism. The recent tendency of historians to neglect this fact only reveals the strong hold that Nelson's original historical evaluation still has on the field's leading scholars. Perhaps more than anything else Jacobsen's unwarranted reworking of the most recognizable eyewitness account associated with interracialism at the Azusa Street revival demonstrates the need for a more comprehensive historical and ecclesiological study of Holiness-Pentecostalism in the area of racial and ethnic relations.[23]

Bishop C. H. Mason and the Roots of the Church of God in Christ (Bakersfield, CA: Pneuma Life, 1996), 45.

20. Douglas Jacobsen, *Thinking in the Spirit: Theologies of the Early Pentecostal Movement* (Bloomington, Ind.: Indiana University Press, 2003).

21. Ibid., 79.

22. Ibid., 261. Frank Bartleman's wording was, "The 'color line' was washed away in the blood."

23. Two recent dissertations reveal the same marked dependence on the dominant historiographical view. See Vivian Eilythia Deno, "Holy Ghost Nation: Race, Gender, and Working-Class Pentecostalism, 1906-1926" (Ph.D. diss., University of California, Irvine, 2002), 23, 28, 35 and 51; Gastón Espinosa, "Borderland Religion: Los Angeles and the Origins of the Latino Pentecostal Movement in the U.S., Mexico, and Puerto Rico, 1900-1945" (Ph.D. diss., University of California, Santa Barbara, 1999), 85, 106. It should be noted that Espinosa makes one reference to the "blood of Jesus," a common allusion to entire sanctification, washing away the color-line at the Azusa Street revival. His use of this phrase, however, does not indicate an appreciation of its holiness background or its connection to sanctified unity ecclesiology (81). In all fairness to Espinosa, he does claim that his interest in Pentecostalism is historical and not theological.

More nuanced positions have been put forward by Cecil M. Robeck, Charles E. Jones and Dale T. Irvin.[24] Robeck has recognized that Seymour became disaffected with the Pentecostal movement as it splintered along racial lines.[25] Out of his deep pain, Robeck surmises, Seymour modulated his earlier position on glossolalia as the sign of Spirit baptism. He now argued for it as a sign to be included with a strong ethical component in the life of the Spirit-filled believer. He rightly notes the importance of Wesleyan sanctification to Seymour's pentecostal matrix as well as Seymour's reiteration of his holiness roots. But Robeck leaves the discussion there and does not attempt to demonstrate how Seymour's views on interracialism were rooted in radical holiness ecclesiology.

Charles E. Jones provides a helpful historical perspective by explaining the important connection between the multiethnic Southern California and Arizona Holiness Association and Azusa Street. However, he does not explore the actual theology of this Wesleyan holiness group, or the larger context of the radical Holiness movement. Outside of demonstrating that many of the Azusa Street participants were already comfortable with interracial fellowship and black leadership, Jones fails to provide any intellectual architecture for the practice of sanctified unity at the revival. Finally, Dale Irvin argues most persuasively for the connection between the holiness roots of the Azusa Street participants, especially Seymour, and the demonstration of sanctified unity, including interracialism, that occurred there between 1906 and 1909. While his instincts are correct in observing the critical contribution of holiness theology, above all the link between sanctification and unity, he only touches on the deep ecclesiological reservoir undergirding sanctified unity in the radical Holiness movement. Furthermore, he still wants to follow the argument enunciated by Nelson that the chief cause of interracialism at Azusa was Spirit baptism. "Participants in the 1906 revival found in this trans-linguistic experience of the baptism of the Holy Spirit both a sign and a means of bringing down the walls of separation that divide the global human community."[26]

---

24. Cecil M. Robeck, Jr., "William J. Seymour and 'The Bible Evidence'," in *Initial Evidence: Historical and Biblical Perspectives on the Pentecostal Doctrine of Spirit Baptism*, ed. Gary B. McGee (Peabody, Mass.: Hendrickson, 1991), 72-95; Cecil M. Robeck, Jr., "Historical Roots of Racial Unity and Division in American Pentecostalism," unpublished paper, n.d.; Charles E. Jones, "The 'Color Line' Washed Away in the Blood? In the Holiness Church, at Azusa Street, and Afterward," *Wesleyan Theological Journal* 34 (Fall 1999): 252-265; Dale T. Irvin, "'Drawing All Together in One Bond of Love': The Ecumenical Vision of William J. Seymour and the Azusa Street Revival," *Journal of Pentecostal Theology* 6 (April 1995): 13-24.

25. Three times whites broke away from the Apostolic Faith Mission between 1906 and 1911. The stated reason for each separation involved a theological controversy, but that the breaks occurred along racial lines suggests that racial prejudice played a role in the divisions.

A sort of third take on the ecclesiological contribution to the socially heterodox community at Azusa Street has been presented in Grant Wacker's book, *Heaven Below: Early Pentecostalism and American Culture.*[27] Wacker makes a nod towards the dominant historiographical position and gives tribute to the work of the Spirit in breaking down the walls of racial prejudice. But unlike the aforementioned scholars, he notes that the editors of *The Apostolic Faith* paper, William J. Seymour and Clara Lum, also connect the practice of interracialism to the "power of Christ's blood, or anticipation of Christ's return."[28] Wacker is on the right course but does not comment on the link between these ideas and radical holiness ecclesiology. Thus, he does not take into consideration the important connection between Seymour's adoption of sanctified unity ecclesiology, especially its interracial and multiethnic dimensions, and his application of it to the Azusa Street revival. This leads Wacker to conclude that interracial theology "played a slight role in [Seymour's] theological thinking."[29]

African-American Historical Perspectives

Finally, the black Christian tradition played a significant role in the development of interracial fellowship within holiness-pentecostal communities. Bringing an end to racism and the full integration of blacks within American society always has been a predominant function and goal of the black churches. Peter J. Paris's *The Social Teaching of the Black Churches* argues that this is the chief contribution of the black Christian tradition.

> Their raison d'etre is inextricably tied to the function of opposing the beliefs and practices of racism by proclaiming the biblical view of humanity as they have appropriated it, that is, the equality of all persons under God. Thus their moral aim is theologically grounded. The doctrine of human equality under God is, for them, the final authority for all matters pertaining to faith, thought, and practice.[30]

In general, then, African Americans were always amicable to a union of the races in the public sphere. It is true that after the Reconstruction period many blacks moved to form separate churches and ecclesiastical organizations. But this must be understood as a reaction to the segregationist impulse that was leading white America to enact Jim Crow legislation across

---

26. Irvin, "Drawing All Together," 27. Vinson Synan & Charles R. Fox, Jr. follow a similar path in their book, *William J. Seymour: Pioneer of the Azusa Street Revival* (Alachua, FL.: Bridge-Logos, 2012).
27. Grant Wacker, *Heaven Below: Early Pentecostalism and American Culture* (Cambridge, Mass.: Harvard University Press, 2001).
28. Ibid., 228.
29. Ibid., 234.
30. Peter J. Paris, *The Social Teaching of the Black Churches* (Philadelphia, Pa.: Fortress, 1985), 14.

the nation.[31] So the impediment to interracial fellowship in American churches is best understood as a white problem, not a black one.[32] While it has been widely acknowledged, very little has been said regarding the theological contributions of the black Christian tradition to the Holiness-Pentecostal movement.[33]

This discussion leads to the question of pentecostal origins. In the main the debate has focused around two figures: Charles Parham and William Seymour. Parham, who is white, is credited with developing the distinctively pentecostal doctrine of Spirit baptism with speaking in tongues considered the Bible evidence. Seymour, who is black, is credited with leading the Azusa Street revival from which most pentecostal churches trace their origins. Moreover, the unique practice of multiethnic worship at the revival is viewed as determinative of the real work of the Spirit. This key aspect of Azusa Street has caused some to posit that the origins of Pentecostalism are more decidedly black than white. Since the black Christian tradition has consistently desired an end to racism and sought the creation of an integrative church it is concluded that black church theology is the primary motive behind racial inclusion at the Apostolic Faith Mission.

Without wanting to dispute the theological contribution that the black Christian tradition made to the outbreak of interracialism at the Azusa Street revival, this dissertation contends that radical holiness theology was more instrumental to the socially heterodox fellowship that unfolded there between 1906 and 1909. The writings of William J. Seymour in *The Apostolic Faith* paper are critical to this evaluation. That he was an African American, born to slave parents, was foundational to the atmosphere of racial equality that existed during the revival. In that sense, those who argue for the black origins of pentecostalism have a point. But his ecclesiology is altogether something different than what one might expect out of the black Christian tradition. There is not a word about the "Fatherhood of God and the brotherhood of man" in his writings, the theological basis from which the African Methodist and Baptist churches argued for an end to racial segregation.[34] Clearly, the influence of black religion on the Los Angeles reviv-

---

31. August Meier, *Negro Thought in America 1880-1915: Racial Ideologies in the Age of Booker T. Washington* (Ann Arbor, Mich.: The University of Michigan Press, 1969), 13.

32. One sympathetic white writer, Judge Albion W. Tourgee stated, "So far as the peaceful and Christian solution of the race problem is concerned, indeed, I am inclined to think that the only education required is that of the *white* race. The hate, the oppression, the injustice are all on our side." See Ronald C. White, Jr., *Liberty and Justice for All: Racial Reform and the Social Gospel (1877-1925)* (San Francisco: Harper & Row, 1990), 8.

33. See Clemmons, *Bishop C. H. Mason,* 57; Clemmons, "True Koinonia," 53; Sanders, *Empowerment Ethics,* 29; Nelson, "For Such a Time," 157.

34. Edward L. Wheeler, *Uplifting the Race: The Black Minister in the New South 1865-1902* (Lanham, Mass.: University Press of America, 1986), 45-50.

al did not come from the elite black clergy.[35] The source of black religion's influence must be found in black folk religion.

Black folk religion was the religion of the downtrodden. But while it was powerful in its influence, it was unable to systematize its theological development.[36] So it is no surprise to discover that Seymour, who arises out of the black folk tradition, acquired his theology of interracialism from another source. This is not difficult to believe since the sources of his theological belief system are relatively easy to detect. An evaluation of Seymour's *The Doctrines and Discipline of the Azusa Street Apostolic Faith Mission of Los Angeles, Cal*, written in 1915, reveals that he "incorporated twenty-four 'Articles of Religion' from the Methodist Episcopal Church into the document."[37] Similarly, the early editions of *The Apostolic Faith* demonstrate a faithful conveyance of Charles Parham's teaching on Spirit baptism that Seymour learned as a student in Houston, Texas.[38] Finally, his writing on holiness issues shows a marked dependence on the writings of F. G. Smith, a Church of God Reformation Movement teacher and editor of the church's publication *Gospel Trumpet*.[39] Taking this into account, it is no surprise to learn that his ecclesiology owes a great debt to his radical holiness background.

The contribution of this insight should cause us to pause and evaluate, once again, the origins of pentecostalism. Plainly, the picture is even more complex than has been previously argued. That the African-American participants at Azusa Street brought with them a legacy of interracial hope is unquestionable. But their radical holiness background also exposed them to a particular interracial and multiethnic ecclesiology, which this monograph terms sanctified unity. Sanctified unity ecclesiology proved effective

---

35. This is not to suggest that Seymour was not aware of the theological reflection occurring within the ranks of the elite black clergy. The familiarity with a wide array of theology that his writings reflect, his probable relationship with the college educated Charles P. Jones and his constant pursuit of biblical truth make it likely that, at a minimum, he had some knowledge of elite black theology at the turn of the century.

36. Acts 10:34, "God is no respecter of persons," was a favorite passage used by adherents to black folk religion to argue against white prejudice. See Donald Mathews, *Religion in the Old South* (Chicago: The University of Chicago Press, 1977), 219; Milton C. Sernett, *Black Religion and American Evangelicalism* (Metuchen, N.J.: Scarecrow Press, 1975), 108.

37. Robeck, "William J. Seymour," 83.

38. See *The Apostolic Faith* (Los Angeles) "The Apostolic Faith Movement," (September 1906): 2; *The Apostolic Faith* (Los Angeles) "The Elder Brother," (October 1906), 2.

39. Cheryl J. Sanders notes that a "point-by-point comparison of the September 1906 edition of Seymour's periodical *Apostolic Faith* with *What the Bible Teaches*, a compilation of early writings by F. G. Smith . . . reveals striking similarities." See Sanders, *Saints in Exile*, 31.

in bringing people together across the lines of color and ethnicity. That William Seymour and other black holiness participants in Los Angeles adopted a theology that caused Christians, especially whites, to die to real prejudices, in retrospect, only makes sense.

Chapter One, "The Radical Holiness Movement," introduces the reader to the emergence of holiness radical churches and associations from the larger Holiness movement. It explains the social context of the day, especially as it relates to African-Americans and their relationship to the larger dominant Caucasian culture of segregationism. The chapter lays out for the reader the personal and organizational connections between holiness radical groups spanning from the Carolinas through the upper South and Midwest and extending across the nation to Southern California. Chapter Two, "Theological Background to Sanctified Unity Ecclesiology," explores the connections between the historic development of Wesleyan theology in the United States and the emergence of interracial churches, which I refer to more theologically as "sanctified unity ecclesiology." Chapter Three, "Sanctified Unity Ecclesiology: The Heart of the Radical Holiness Message," defines the ecclesiology of sanctified unity. At its core, the radical Holiness movement called for a restoration of the original unity of the New Testament church, both corporately and communally. Chapter Four, "Living Holiness on the Other Side of the Color Line," tells the story of interracial churches from the perspective of the holiness radical saints. It relates the counter culture nature of their church fellowships, their efforts to birth and sustain interracial churches during the Jim Crow era, and their limitations. Chapter Five, "Sanctified Unity Ecclesiology and the Azusa Street Revival," argues that the leadership and participants at Azusa Street shared the common background of the radical Holiness movement and, as a result, brought with them into the revival an ecclesiology of sanctified unity. The interracial atmosphere at the Azusa Street Mission then was more a result of an already developed ecclesiology that the participants shared and the strong leadership of William J. Seymour. This is an alternative view to the dominant historiographical position that sees the doctrine of Spirit baptism with the Bible evidence of speaking in tongues as the key to understanding the interracial environment that existed during much of the Azusa Street Revival. My view is that Spirit baptism worked as a complement to the interracial aspects of sanctified unity ecclesiology.

Chapter One

The Radical Holiness Movement

The emergence of interracial and multiethnic churches within the radical[1] Holiness movement at the turn of the twentieth century marks one of the most compelling epochs in the history of race and ethnic relations in the American church. Almost without warning thousands of ordinary people, white, black and brown, beholden in large part to the same racial and ethnic prejudices exhibited in the Jim and Jane Crow America in which they lived, suddenly found themselves in fraternal communion with each other. Soon to be stigmatized in their local communities and often confronted with a violent racism meant to intimidate them into silence, many radical Holiness proponents fearlessly continued to preach on. For almost a generation, from the beginning of the Church of God Reformation Movement in 1880 to the end of the Azusa Street revival in 1909, they practiced what they preached, wedding the biblical concepts of holiness and unity together to produce a sanctified unity ecclesiology that fostered interracial and multi-ethnic fellowship and broke down the walls of denominationalism. They believed, *ipso facto*, that the biblical "Church of God" meant the unity of all Christians. Inherent in the ecclesiology of sanctified unity, then, was the erasing of denominational, racial and ethnic lines. Also basic to their message was the belief that in the rediscovery of the Church of God the restoration of the New Testament church had come to pass.[2]

---

1. The term "radical" is used to denote a core set of holiness groups which separated from the larger Holiness movement over the issue of ecclesiology. Holiness radicals argued that biblical holiness produces one, united Church of God. A subset of radical holiness groups went on to define unity communally and so were inclusive of all races, ethnicities and nationalities.

2. Josephine M. Washburn describes the conclusion made among radical holiness workers in Southern California about the connection between holiness and the restoration of the New Testament church. "First, it had been made quite clear that the

It is important to note that not every radical holiness group practiced sanctified unity ecclesiology to the same degree, nor did every individual important to the history of sanctified unity ecclesiology break away from the larger Holiness movement to join a radical holiness fellowship. As a result, the history of the participants who contributed to the formation of sanctified unity ecclesiology cannot be separated into easily defined categories.

Sanctified unity ecclesiology operated on two levels within the radical Holiness movement. At its foundational level it worked to bring an end to denominationalism and through holiness and unity restore the biblical "Church of God." Every fellowship of sanctified believers that joined the holiness radicals eventually ended all denominational ties and formed an independent holiness work. But to different degrees each of these groups took a second step that further delineated their ecclesiology from the nation-wide Holiness movement. Crossing racial, ethnic and national lines, radical holiness fellowships began to define unity in a way that was counter to the late nineteenth-century American ethos. During a time when Jim and Jane Crow were increasingly shutting down the points of social contact between different races and ethnicities, even in mainstream Christianity, radical holiness groups opened their doors to all Christians. The Church of God Reformation Movement and the Southern California and Arizona Holiness Association, for example, profoundly implemented both levels of sanctified unity ecclesiology within their bodies. On the other hand, the Church of God (Holiness) moved barely beyond the foundational level. Nevertheless, each fellowship of holiness radicals, and some individuals who never did leave the "Babylon" of denominationalism but participated in the saints' revivals, made important contributions to the conceptual nature of sanctified unity ecclesiology.

Social Context

It is difficult today to comprehend the profound influence that segregationist policies and attitudes played in the shaping of American culture at the turn of the twentieth century. Yet it is necessary to have some idea of the impact of Jim Crowism if the revolutionary nature of the radical Holiness movement is to be appreciated. The full implementation of sanctified unity ecclesiology demanded great courage on the part of the saints. But it also required a perspective that challenged the dominant mythos of American culture: the superiority of the white race.

Most historians mark the 1890s as the beginning of Jim and Jane Crow.[3] The persistent and incorrigible racist attitudes of most white Americans

---

establishing of the New Testament or Christ's Church, was founded on Holiness or Sanctification." See Washburn, *History and Reminiscences*, 58.

and the dismantling of the policy of Reconstruction in the Compromise of 1877, meant the prospect for social, economic and political equality for African Americans, and by extension other ethnic groups, was fixed long before the 1890s. Still, an unprecedented window of opportunity for blacks did open after the Civil War and did not completely close until the last decade of the nineteenth century. Ronald C. White has characterized race relations in the two decades preceding the 1890s as a "period of some fluidity and uncertainty."[4] It was during this period that the radical Holiness movement started. That it persisted for an additional twenty years while the grip of Jim Crow tightened and choked the life out of the black aspiration for social equality is testimony to the power of its message and the resolve of its followers.

The subjugation of African Americans to a social status just above slavery began in earnest in 1890. The state of Mississippi led the way by revising the state Constitution in 1890 to disenfranchise blacks. Along with requiring a poll tax and certain residence and property qualifications, they also called for literacy and Constitution tests for their citizens before they were allowed to vote. The revisions also included the infamous "grandfather clause" allowing whites to circumvent the new requirements since their grandfathers had been eligible to vote.[5] By 1895 South Carolina followed Mississippi's lead in revising the state's constitution and thirteen years later most of the Southern states had joined them.[6] The Supreme Court provided its *imprimatur* in *Williams v. Mississippi* (1898) when it upheld the 1890 Constitutional revisions made in Mississippi and ended any immediate hope that blacks might regain their voting rights.[7]

In 1883 proponents of segregationism were also aided by the Supreme Court's decision to overturn the Civil Rights Act of 1875. The measure had protected African Americans from discrimination in public spaces.[8] Four years later the first state law was passed segregating whites and blacks on trains.[9] By the end of the nineteenth century the races were separated in every public institution and place, including public education. And in *Plessey v. Ferguson* (1896) the doctrine of "separate but equal" became the justifying cry for advocates of Jim Crow everywhere.

The lynching of African Americans during this period provides another way to judge the deteriorating situation in the country. In 1889 a total of

---

3. Wheeler, *Uplifting the Race*, 77; White, *Liberty and Justice*, 10; Leon F. Litwick, *Trouble in Mind: Black Southerners in the Age of Jim Crow* (New York: Alfred A. Knopf, 1998), xiv.

4. Ibid., 10.

5. Wheeler, *Uplifting the Race*, 77.

6. Meier, *Negro Thought*, 162.

7. H. Shelton Smith, *In His Image, But . . .: Racism in Southern Religion, 1780-1910* (Durham, N.C.: Duke University Press, 1972), 264.

8. Meier, *Negro Thought*, 9; Smith, *In His Image*, 263.

9. White, *Liberty and Justice*, 11.

175 people were lynched in the United States. The split between the numbers of whites lynched, 80, and blacks, 95, was nearly even. The next year, 1890, took a precipitous turn for the worse in the legal and physical protection of African Americans. Out of a total of 91 lynchings, blacks numbered an astonishing 88. Lynching statistics demonstrate that over the next thirty years African Americans made up a disproportionate number of those who were lynched. The number of blacks that were murdered through lynching only tells part of the story. The social limitations placed on African Americans out of fear of "Judge Lynch" can never be calculated.[10]

The country also witnessed a surge in race riots at the turn of the twentieth century. Besides the well-known southern race riots that broke out in Wilmington, North Carolina in 1898 and Atlanta, Georgia in 1906, race riots were also experienced in New York City in 1900 and Springfield, Illinois in 1908.[11] Theologians and scientists also contributed to the progressively hostile environment for African Americans. Books such as Charles Carroll's *The Negro a Beast* (1900) and Robert W. Shufeldt's *The Negro: A Menace to American Civilization* (1907) drew upon the work of biblical exegetes and biologists to consign blacks to the bottom rung of civilization, and lower. And when Thomas Dixon's *The Clansmen* was made into the movie *The Birth of a Nation* in 1915, the ideology undergirding Jim and Jane Crowism had made its way into mainstream American entertainment.[12] Indeed, as the North and South worked towards reconciliation, the North not only capitulated to the segregationist demands of the South but drew its own color line throughout Northern society. At the turn of the century the attitudes of most Northerners had hardened against bringing the freedmen into social equality with whites. In the words of the historian August Meier, "public opinion in the North had come to feel that Negroes were an inferior race, unfitted for the franchise, and that white domination was justified."[13]

Historical Background

The radical Holiness movement can be rightly said to spring out of the spiritual travails of one man, Daniel Sidney Warner, who felt called of God to reestablish the church of the New Testament. After converting to the Church of God (Winebrennerian) movement Warner served as a minister inside its ranks for a decade. Central to its message was the doctrine of the church. "It was agreed, as the unanimous sense of the meeting: First. There

---

10. Ibid., 11-12.
11. Jean Russell notes that "there were six major race riots between 1908 and 1920." See Jean Russell, *God's Lost Cause: A Study of the Church and the Racial Problem* (London: SCM, 1968), 84.
12. Meier, *Negro Thought*, 161.
13. Ibid., 21.

is but one true church; namely the Church of God. Secondly. That it is the bounden duty of all God's people to belong to her, and none else."[14]

The experience of entire sanctification became the second important doctrinal insight in Warner's developing theology. Initially opposed to the "second blessing," he began to warm up under the influence of his sanctified wife, and his father-in-law, who was a part of the Holiness movement. In the summer of 1877 Warner began to probe more deeply into the experience, finally placing all on the altar on the fifth day of July. "Hallelujah, it is done!" was the response he recorded in his diary.[15]

The message of holiness immediately became a central focus of Warner's preaching. Opposed to the Wesleyan doctrine of entire sanctification, the Church of God (Winebrennerian) quickly brought Warner up on charges and made him stand trial. By January 30, 1878, the pastor had been stripped of his license to preach on the count of "dividing the church."[16] The next day Warner reached a resolution on the whole matter which he later entered into his diary.

> On the 31st of last January the Lord showed me that holiness could never prosper upon sectarian soil encumbered by human creeds and party names, and he gave me a new commission to join holiness and all truth together and build up the apostolic church of the living God. Praise his name! I will obey him.[17]

Originally interpreting his spiritual revelation to apply only to direct participation in denominations, he soon concluded that any organization that made membership in a denomination a prerequisite for fellowship should also be opposed. In short, Warner believed that any working relationship with a denomination was unbiblical. He opposed the sectarian nature of denominationalism, contending that it contravened Jesus' prayer for Christian unity in John 17. Accordingly, he withdrew from the Indiana Holiness Association when it rejected his proposal to change the wording of its constitution from an association which "consists of members of various Christian organizations" to, it "shall consist of and seek to cooperate with all true Christians everywhere."[18] The rejection of Warner's proposal marked the beginning of the Church of God Reformation Movement, later located in Anderson, Indiana. The controversy hinged on different conceptions of ecclesiology. The Indiana Holiness Association, and by extension the National Holiness Association, believed that the doctrine of entire sanctification ap-

---

14. Smith, *Holiness and Unity*, 38.

15. Ibid., 52.

16. Melvin E. Dieter, *The Holiness Revival of the Nineteenth Century* (Lanham, M.D.: Scarecrow Press, 1996), 209.

17. John W. V. Smith, *Heralds of a Brighter Day*
(Anderson, Ind.: Gospel Trumpet Company, 1955), 38.

18. Dieter, *Holiness Revival*, 216.

plied to the individual and not the corporate church. Warner disagreed, understanding the application of holiness to the church, individually and corporately, as the central message of the Bible. A short time later, Warner and the men and women now coalescing around him brought their ecclesiological conclusions into the public light: "we wish to announce to all that we wish to cooperate with all Christians, as such in saving souls—but forever withdraw from all organisms that uphold and endorse sects and denominations in the body of Christ."[19]

Warner's message grounded the Winebrennerian conception of the Church of God in the holiness doctrine of entire sanctification. The original Church of God, he maintained, kept its unity as a result of its holiness. God's design for a united church had not changed even though man's innate selfishness continued to divide the church. Only the experience of the "double cure" could remove the self-centered nature from the individual and make unity possible. He reasoned, therefore, that the path of return to New Testament ecclesiology lay in the application of holiness to the body of Christ.

As editor of the *Gospel Trumpet*, the organ for the Church of God Reformation Movement, Warner had a megaphone for propagating his message throughout the Midwest. The message found a receptive audience among native whites, recent immigrants from Europe, African Americans and other marginalized ethnic groups. The formation of church bodies based on holiness and unity, or what this study calls sanctified unity ecclesiology, rested on a particular reading of Scripture which coalesced around John 17 and Gal 3:28.[20] Sanctified unity ecclesiology advocated a specific understanding of the church which called for all sanctified Christians to fellowship together as one Church of God. A radical concept in any period of American history, its conception at the end of the Reconstruction period and the beginning of Jim and Jane Crowism pushed these radical Holiness groups way out of the mainstream of American church life.

Warner continued to attend regional Holiness conferences where participants were receptive to his views on the church. In 1880, at the Western Union Holiness Convention held in Jacksonville, Illinois, he was a featured speaker. His message was of central importance since the question of ecclesiology was uppermost in the minds of many advocates of holiness. Also attending the convention was John P. Brooks. Eleven years later Brooks would write the *Divine Church* (1891), the definitive presentation of the Church of God concept as derived from sanctified living. Melvin E. Dieter argues persuasively that Warner and Brooks could not have failed to meet during the convention, if not earlier within holiness circles.[21] As Brooks's ideas on the church continued to develop over the next decade they bore a

---

19. Ibid., 217.
20. Sanctified unity ecclesiology is fully developed in chapter three.
21. Dieter, *Holiness Revival*, 217-221.

striking similarity to Warner's and the Church of God Reformation Movement. As editor of the *Good Way*, Brooks's writings supported those working for ecclesiastical independence then unfolding in Illinois, Missouri and other Midwestern states in the late 1870s and into the 1880s. In time the Southwestern Holiness Association, a regional franchise of the National Holiness Association, morphed into the Church of God (Holiness). Brooks played a key role in the formation of this radical holiness church, and by extension, so did the ideas of Daniel Warner. Clarence E. Cowen, Church of God (Holiness) historian, underscores Warner's influence by noting that "its [Church of God (Anderson)] beliefs are identical with the Church of God (Holiness) with the exception that it believes footwashing is an ordinance and does not believe in the millennial reign of Christ."[22] A generation later, in 1917, when Church of God (Holiness) leader A. M. Kiergan reflected back on the beginning days, he unintentionally communicated the strong influence of Warner's radical Holiness ecclesiology:

> The phrase 'one true church' was employed to characterize the primitive church, the church the apostles knew from the church of sect of every form and age; and was designed to apply to the reborn New Testament church of the independent Holiness movement. The conception was that no sect could be the 'one true church' and for the same reason 'the one true church' cannot be a sect.[23]

While there are bits and pieces of information which demonstrate that the Church of God (Holiness) wrestled with the prospects of crossing the segregationist line in American society, there is little evidence that the church formed interracial or multiethnic fellowships and placed minorities in positions of leadership. Instead, they progressed very little beyond the foundational level of sanctified unity ecclesiology. Nevertheless, they are an important part of the story on two accounts. First, the aforementioned John P. Brooks presented one the most cogent arguments against denominationalism and for the Church of God concept in his important book the *Divine Church*. And secondly, the group provided a link between the teachings of Warner and the Southern California and Arizona Holiness Association.[24]

As the city of Los Angeles began to experience its first wave of phenomenal growth at the end of the nineteenth century, many of its new immigrants came from the Midwest. With the new arrivals also came the message of holiness. Three evangelists originally from Illinois, Hardin Wallace, Harry Ashcraft and James Jayns, began preaching the holiness message

---

22. Clarence E. Cowen, *A History of the Church of God (Holiness)*(Overland Park, Kans.: Herald and Banner Press, 1949), 15.
23. Ibid., 41.
24. Dieter reports that out on the field the Church of God Reformation Movement and the Church of God (Holiness) developed a "strong mutual antagonism" for each other despite their shared doctrinal view of the church and holiness. See Dieter, *Holiness Revival*, 224.

sometime before 1880. All three were Methodists. On July 1, 1880 the fruit of their labors was gathered together in the Southern California and Arizona Holiness Association.[25] Anyone who had experienced entire sanctification could belong to the association no matter denominational affiliation. Soon, however, the group's intensive evangelism brought in individuals who had no church home but the association. Since these new converts had no reason, nor desire, to make a denominational church their place of worship, the Holiness association took its first step towards becoming a church. By 1885 the association of holiness groups had its own publication, *The Pentecost*, to reflect its emphasis upon the sanctifying experience of the baptism of the Holy Spirit. In a pattern that would repeat itself all across the nation, the Southern California Holiness movement, as it grew in numbers, and as its criticism of denominationalism became more pronounced, found its access to denominational pulpits severely restricted. Criticized as "come-outers" by those loyal to their denominational church but declaring that they were "put-out," new radical holiness churches formed out of local and regional Holiness associations.

The connection between holiness radicals in Southern California and the Midwest was a strong one. Families originally from the Midwest made the journey back and forth, ensuring a constant flow of information between the two regions. Washburn calls special attention to the harmony and unity that her group and radical holiness groups in Kansas and Illinois felt.[26] Dieter notes that the connection between Warner, Brooks and the leading Holiness families in Southern California should be taken into consideration when studying the "church organization" in these diverse geographic areas.[27] This statement is especially appropriate when the implementation of sanctified unity ecclesiology is considered in the Southern California and Arizona Holiness Association. Seemingly unselfconscious about its inte-

---

25. For an early history of the Southern California and Arizona Holiness Association see Washburn, *History and Reminiscences*; and for a firsthand account see W. B. Shepard, "Come-Out-Ism In California," *The Pentecost* 18th year No. 401 (September 26, 1902), 3.

26. Washburn, *History and Reminiscences*, 289-290.

27. Dieter, *Holiness Revival*, 221. There is a B. A. Washburn who is mentioned in both the Southern California and Illinois Holiness movements. Dieter mentions his involvement in the church question in Southern California and Cowen notes that he played a leading role in an interracial dispute that took place at Pauline Holiness School in Missouri—see footnote 264 in chapter three. Additionally, his article "The Unity of the Spirit" in the December 25, 1886 issue of *The Pentecost* advocated sanctified unity ecclesiology on the basis of John 10:16 and I Corinthians 12:13. The known evidence favors the conclusion that the B. A. Washburn working in the Southern California Holiness movement is the same person that Cowen mentions in his history of the Midwestern based Church of God (Holiness), thus further substantiating the close ties between the two radical holiness groups. See Dieter, *Holiness Revival*, 226; Cowen, *Church of God (Holiness)*, 35.

grated makeup, SCAHA became a truly remarkable example of an interracial and multiethnic church. Even a casual reading of *The Pentecost* reveals a racially-mixed leadership and social structure that was comparable to the Church of God Reformation Movement.

Journal articles published in radical holiness periodicals in one region and republished in the other demonstrate a familiarity, as well, between the West coast and the Midwest. For example, W. B. Shepard's article in *The Pentecost* relating the early history of the Southern California Holiness movement was first published in the *Burning Bush*.[28] In his piece he connected the holiness activity in Chicago with that in Southern California by placing emphasis on what made them unique: their ecclesiology. "The work in Chicago and the work in California are not come-out-ism, but simply church homes."[29] Finally, Washburn reports in her history that through SCAHA's work among blacks in the South they came into contact with an African-American holiness group in North Carolina. The doctrinal stance of both groups was nearly identical and created a sense of unity between the two groups, and brought the disparate radical holiness groups even closer together.[30]

When SCAHA sent out George and Laura Goings, African-American evangelists and leaders within the movement, to spread the holiness message among blacks living in the South, yet another relationship formed between Southern California and the middle part of the nation. On the invitation of Joanna P. Moore, white holiness educator among southern blacks, George and Laura Goings made Nashville, Tennessee the headquarters for their work.[31] The Goingses also formed working relationships with J. O. McClurkan, founder of the Pentecostal Mission, also in Nashville, and C. P. Jones, co-founder of the Church of God of Christ, and eventual bishop of the Church of Christ (Holiness) U.S.A.[32] Later, Goings would arrange for the

---

28. Shepherd was an associate pastor of the Pentecostal Church of the Nazarene in California and a special envoy for Phineas Bresee at the General Holiness Assembly in Chicago in 1901. His exposure to members of the Metropolitan Church Association(MCA) during his stay in Chicago converted him to their particular brand of radical holiness. He later became editor of the MCA organ *Burning Bush*. His connection to the radical Holiness movement in Southern California and the MCA, and the close ties to God's Bible School and the ministries of Knapp and Rees in the first years of the MCA demonstrate the interconnectedness and fluidity of the radical Holiness movement. See William Kostlevy, "Nor Silver, Nor Gold: The Burning Bush Movement and the Communitarian Holiness Vision" (Ph.D., diss., University of Notre Dame, 1996), 121.

29. Shepard, "Come-Out-Ism," 3.

30. Washburn, *History and Reminiscences*, 289-290. This is a likely reference to the Pentecostal Holiness Church work in North Carolina that also followed an ecclesiology of sanctified unity.

31. Ibid., 88-89.

President of SCAHA, George Teel, to stay at McClurkan's Pentecostal Mission during a tour of the holiness work in the South. That McClurkan and Teel would have met during this time is likely given the stature of the guest from California. The two men shared a similar theological understanding of the faith, both were passionate about spreading the holiness message throughout the South and each considered entire sanctification to be the remedy of racial, ethnic and regional prejudices. Still, there is no documentary evidence that the two men did in fact meet.

William A. Washington, likewise, is a good example of the close working relationships that existed between the different radical holiness groups in Middle Tennessee at the turn of the twentieth century. Reared a Baptist in the state of Mississippi, he experienced sanctification when he was twelve through the Church of God in Christ (COGIC). An active member of COGIC from 1895 to 1908, he left after the "tongues movement" became a significant feature of the church. Soon thereafter he joined the Nashville District of the Holiness Church under the direction of George Goings and within a few years became an elder and chairman of the church. Later, he rejoined Charles Price Jones and became bishop of the Western Diocese and vice-president of the national convention of the Church of Christ (Holiness) U.S.A. He died in May, 1949 in Los Angeles.[33]

The Pentecostal Mission originated in the year 1898 under the leadership of James Octavius McClurkan. McClurkan received his sanctification experience while still a Cumberland Presbyterian pastor in San Jose, California. Highly respected as the pastor of one of the largest churches in San Jose, he was invited to a local Methodist meeting to hear the evangelist Beverly Carradine. Before taking up an itinerant ministry the irrepressible Carradine had created a larger than life reputation within the Methodist Episcopal Church, South, as an advocate for personal and social holiness. Carradine never did leave the Methodist church but played a significant role in the emergence of radical holiness. Including McClurkan, at least three significant radical holiness leaders received their sanctifying experience under his evangelistic ministry.[34] McClurkan received his sanctification experience in 1895.[35]

---

32. George Goings later joined his holiness efforts with C. P. Jones' work and became a member of the Church of Christ (Holiness) U.S.A. See Sherry Sherrod DuPree, "In the Sanctified Holiness Pentecostal Charismatic Movement," *Pneuma* 23 (Spring 2001): 102.

33. Otho B. Cobbins, ed., *History of Church of Christ (Holiness) U.S.A. 1895-1965* (New York: Vantage Press, 1966), 39-44; *Southern Pentecost*, no. 677 (November 23, 1911): 21; Washburn, *History and Reminiscences*, 421-425.

34. The other two were Edwin Harvey, leader of the Metropolitan Church Association in Chicago and Milwaukee and Ambrose Crumpler, leader of the Pentecostal Holiness Church in North Carolina.

McClurkan chose Nashville as his base of operations because of the centrality of its location within the South. He believed that the holiness work in Middle Tennessee needed to be organized if it was to have any permanence.[36] The reason behind the formation of the Pentecostal Mission was to keep the message of holiness alive in the denominational churches.[37] The opening of the Pentecostal Literary and Bible Training School on November 5, 1901 provided McClurkan the opportunity to expand the reach of the Pentecostal Mission and shape the future leaders of radical holiness in Middle Tennessee and beyond. Such notable holiness workers as Matthew Mack Pinson, Henry G. Rodgers and Leonard P. Adams attended McClurkan's school.[38]

Pinson enrolled in the school in October of 1902. The school, like all holiness schools, believed that students should split their time between study and evangelistic work. Reflecting McClurkan's theological position that entire sanctification removes the divisiveness of racial prejudice, Pinson held mixed-race revivals.[39] Later Pinson would partner with Rodgers in spreading the Pentecostal message in Alabama and Mississippi.[40]

L. P. Adams worked with the predominantly black Church of God in Christ in Memphis, Tennessee. When Adams later sought a ministerial license with the Assemblies of God, letters of inquiry were sent to Charles Mason, head of the COGIC, and Elder E. M. Page, overseer for the COGIC's work in Texas and Oklahoma, for their judgment on his character. Some people were alleging that Adams had been disreputable in his handling of

---

35. William J. Strickland and H. Ray Dunning, *J. O. McClurkan: His Life, His Theology, and Selections from His Writings* (Nashville, Tenn.: Trevecca Press, 1998), 25-26.

36. Ibid., 28, 32.

37. McClurkan's view of entire sanctification was slightly heterodox when compared with the prevailing views within radical holiness circles. He favored the teaching of a crisis moment when one received the experience of entire sanctification, but also held that there were subsequent experiences to the "second blessing" where the sanctified believer underwent a "deeper death to self" to grow in more perfect maturity. Ibid., 90.

38. Gary D. McElhany, "The South Aflame: A History of the Assemblies of God in the Gulf Region, 1901-1940" (Ph.D, diss., Mississippi State University, 1996), 91, 95; Paul S. Carter, *Heritage of Holiness* (Self-Published, 1991), 15. All three men later joined the Pentecostal movement.

39. During one tent revival in Columbus, Mississippi, in 1903, several African-American men left their designated seating and sat in the section reserved for whites. When complaints arrived threatening to burn down the tent and bring an end to the revival, Pinson, at the suggestion of black leaders, returned the revival back to its segregated seating pattern. See McElhany, "The South Aflame," 92.

40. Pinson and Rodgers also had contact with Charles H. Mason, head of the Church of God in Christ. Both men attended pentecostal revival services in 1907 at Mason's church which led to their own Spirit baptisms. McElhany reports that Pinson then left Memphis immediately and traveled to Nashville to discuss the event with McClurkan. Ibid., 96.

money. In response to the inquiry Mason wrote a letter on January 29, 1932, describing his working relationship with Adams thus, "Yes for many years Elder Adams laboured [sic] [with] us. We enjoyed many days of sweet communion together. Now as to little rumors. I too have heard but I know nothing of a truth. I can only say as the Lord says, Prove all things and hold fast that, that's good."[41] Dated six days earlier, on January 23, 1932, Page noted that he had "Known Him [Adams] for Prehaps [sic] 28 or thirty years and have been Associated with him from time to time, and he did Carry Credentials with the Church of God in Christ. I wish to say during this time I have never Known any thing in Elder Adams Life w [sic] That would Disqualify him for the Ministry."[42]

As a result of the many contacts between white and black saints in Nashville, Memphis and surrounding areas, Tennessee represented a significant hub where holiness radicals favored the implementation of sanctified unity ecclesiology in the South.

Martin Wells Knapp's ministry in Cincinnati, Ohio, became another hub in the ever expanding radical Holiness movement where sanctified unity ecclesiology was taught and practiced. Born in 1853 to parents doing pioneer work in rural Michigan for the Methodist Episcopal Church, Knapp attended the Methodist school Albion College at age sixteen.[43] After college he served as a Methodist minister and in 1882 "prayed through" until he received the experience of entire sanctification. Knapp described his Spirit baptism using the allegorical language that he later made famous in his book *Out of Egypt into Canaan*:

> In November, 1882, I permitted the Lord to lead me to Kadesh-Barnea, on the borders of the promised land. By His grace I then and there entered the land, receiving the blessed baptism of the Spirit that cleanses from inbred sin and fills with perfect love.[44]

The publication of *The Revivalist* began in 1888.[45] By 1891 Knapp had relocated to Cincinnati, Ohio, positioning his ministry on the border between the Northern and Southern Holiness movements. Interestingly, John P. Brooks had given a speech a decade before at a Holiness conference in Cincinnati entitled "What are the Chief Hindrances to the Progress of the Work of Sanctification Among Believers." The chief cause given by Brooks was the inherent denominational problem of sectarianism. He went on to

---

41. L. P. Adams file at the Assemblies of God's Flower Pentecostal Heritage Center.
42. L. P. Adams file at the Assemblies of God's Flower Pentecostal Heritage Center.
43. A. M. Hills, *A Hero of Faith and Prayer or Life of Rev. Martin Wells Knapp* (Cincinnati, Ohio: Mrs. Martin Wells Knapp, 1902), 21, 26.
44. Ibid., 54.
45. Renamed *God's Revivalist* in 1901 with Knapp's acceptance of God's literal ownership of all things. This led him to place the name of God at the front end of all his enterprises (e.g. God's Bible School).

call for the "Church of God" concept to be accepted by holiness groups.[46] Initially, Knapp joined with other sanctified workers to form the Central Holiness League which required members to testify to entire sanctification and belong to an evangelical denomination. But as the 1890s progressed Knapp became more disenchanted with the Methodist Episcopal Church and the National Holiness Association. Meeting Seth Rees in 1896, Knapp and the Quaker holiness evangelist soon formed a working relationship that produced a new organization in 1897, the International Holiness Union and Prayer League. The formation of the International Holiness Union and Prayer League essentially brought to an end their relationship with the National Holiness Association. Knapp, Rees and other holiness radicals in Cincinnati became a part of the independent holiness work that was rapidly spreading across the entire nation. The message to leave "dead" churches and join the "Church of God" movement also was broadcast to the 20,000 or more weekly subscribers to *The Revivalist*. Knapp's move towards independence culminated on January 1, 1901 when he officially resigned from the Methodist Episcopal Church.[47]

By the spring of 1900 Knapp and Rees began to forge ties with holiness radicals in Chicago.[48] Duke M. Farson and Edwin L. Harvey, founders of the Metropolitan Church Association (MCA),[49] invited Knapp and Rees to join them for a Holiness convention that opened on March 1, 1901. The MCA had become a bastion of holiness teaching after Farson and Harvey experienced the "second blessing" under the preaching of Beverly Carradine during a holiness revival held at their church in 1897. The 1901 convention quickly turned into a revival that tallied 2,200 people seeking salvation or entire sanctification in just seventy-five days. Knapp became enthralled with the MCA, believing it to be the nearest embodiment of the New Testament church that he had encountered.

> Its pastor and his helpers, abominate fairs, festivals, concerts, and all such worldly things in the Church of God, and demand that their ministers must have the baptism of the Holy Ghost and fire as Jesus requires, and will not tolerate fireless preachers.[50]

Knapp's encounter with MCA saints seemed to invigorate his commitment to restoring the original church in his time. In an article published in *The Revivalist* on December 27, 1900, he wrote,

---

46. Dieter, *Holiness Revival*, 184-185.
47. Kostlevy, "Nor Silver, Nor Gold," 27-32, 90.
48. The articles of MCA leaders began to appear in *The Revivalist* in 1900 and members from the MCA studied at God's Bible School. Ibid., 83-84, 87.
49. The Metropolitan Church Association was known as the Metropolitan Methodist Episcopal Church before it moved out from under the jurisdiction of the Methodist Episcopal Church.
50. As quoted in Kostlevy, "Nor Silver, Nor Gold," 88.

> The mission of the *Revivalist* is to God's people of every name, whether on board the New Testament Church, sailing triumphantly on life's ocean and rescuing sinking seaman on every side, or whether aboard dead and dying Churches, doing their utmost to awaken people to their danger and urge them to loyalty to God.[51]

Tragically, Martin Wells Knapp was dead within a year of writing this piece for *The Revivalist*.[52] The founding of God's Bible School, the International Apostolic Holiness Union[53], *God's Revivalist* and an influential publishing house made Cincinnati one of the vital centers for the radical Holiness movement.[54] Five years after his death his work continued to influence the radical Holiness movement even as some within it accepted the Pentecostal message at the Azusa Street revival in Los Angeles.

The Azusa Street revival brought together in one event representatives from almost every radical Holiness group that practiced some level of sanctified unity ecclesiology. When that is taken into consideration it makes the interracial and multiethnic atmosphere that prevailed during much of the revival more understandable. But it also demonstrates the degree to which holiness radicals worked and participated together during seasons of revivals.

No person exhibited the entangled nature of the radical Holiness movement better than William J. Seymour. Seymour's radical holiness resume included a ministerial license with the Church of God Reformation Movement and a brief time of study at God's Bible School in Cincinnati. Both of these radical holiness centers espoused and practiced an ecclesiology founded on sanctified unity. He also studied under the tutelage of Charles Parham, the first person to teach speaking in tongues as the Bible evidence of the Baptism of the Holy Spirit, and preached alongside him to African-American audiences in Houston, Texas. Parham's overtly racist views did not develop, or at least did not become public, until after he had fallen from grace as the leader of the nascent Pentecostal movement. Before then his admittedly paternalistic approach towards working with African Americans was nevertheless intimate by the standards of the day. Finally, there is

---

51. Ibid., 91.

52. After his unexpected death a falling out occurred between the MCA and those closest to Knapp in Cincinnati. The disagreement revolved around control of Knapp's ministries, with each side claiming that Knapp had appointed them to take over after his death.

53. The International Apostolic Holiness Union was a descendent of the International Holiness Union and Prayer League. The name was changed to emphasize the four main characteristics of their fellowship.

54. Roger Robins notes that A. J. Tomlinson sent reports to *The Revivalist* detailing his missionary work in Tennessee. See Roger Robins, "A. J. Tomlinson: Plainfolk Modernist," in *Portraits of a Generation: Early Pentecostal Leaders*, ed. Grant Wacker (Fayetteville, Ark.: The University of Arkansas Press, 2002), 355.

good, but not conclusive evidence, that Seymour met with Charles P. Jones and Charles H. Mason during a Holiness conference held in Jackson, Mississippi at the end of 1904. Both Jones and Mason believed that holiness and unity should work together to create a church free from racial prejudice.[55] As a result of his many radical Holiness contacts, and his short stint with Parham, Seymour arrived in Los Angeles not only willing to preach the third work of Spirit baptism, but inclined to establish a "Church of God" that was racially and ethnically inclusive.

The opening of the revival at the Apostolic Faith Mission immediately drew upon the surrounding radical holiness groups, many of whom were already committed to sanctified unity ecclesiology. Some members of the Southern California and Arizona Holiness Association became participants at the revival. Josephine Washburn relates several stories demonstrating the animosity that developed between those members of SCAHA who joined the revival and those who did not.[56] The reaction among the leadership of SCAHA towards the revival also was negative. Unlike Charles Parham, however, they did not react negatively towards the interracial and multiethnic services taking place inside the mission, but leveled their criticism at the revival's new pentecostal message. SCAHA rejected the notion that their members had not received the baptism of the Holy Spirit in sanctification and considered the revival's teaching of a third experience to be unbiblical.[57] This position was virtually unanimous among holiness radicals who did not accept the pentecostal message. Importantly, the sanctified unity ecclesiology taught and practiced at Azusa Street did not produce one line of criticism. Indeed, those saints who left SCAHA to join the Apostolic Faith Mission revival contributed to the interracial and multiethnic makeup of the group.

The Metropolitan Church Association also became intimately involved early on with the Azusa Street revival. Two years prior to the beginning of the revival MCA had sent W. E. Shepard to plant a church for the Burning Bush movement in Los Angeles. Shepard already had deep roots in the Holiness movement in Southern California and so was a natural choice. Saved and sanctified under the work of the Southern California and Arizona Holiness Association, and later an associate pastor for the Pentecostal[58] Church of the Nazarene,[59] Shepard now returned to Los Angeles as a representative

---

55. Dale T. Irwin gives a concise summary of the evidence available on the potential meeting between Seymour and Jones. See Dale T. Irwin, "Charles Price Jones: Image of Holiness," in *Portraits of a Generation: Early Pentecostal Leaders*, ed. Grant Wacker (Fayetteville, Ark.: The University of Arkansas Press, 2002), 43-44.

56. Washburn, *History and Reminiscences*, 378-385.

57. Ibid., 377.

58. "Pentecostal" was a part of the original name.

of yet another radical holiness group, this one out of Chicago. After an un-
promising start Shepard returned to Chicago and A. G. and Lillian Garr were
sent in his place. Directly attacking the Nazarene's more "liberal" position
on divorce and remarriage, the Garrs started having some success in building up a following. Shepard again traveled out to Los Angeles, this time
bringing with him Glenn A. Cook. The run of success soon abated and the
Los Angeles MCA struggled for the next two years. By May, 1906 Shepard
had left the MCA work for good, leaving A. G. Garr in charge. The sensation-
al news coverage of the Azusa Street revival convinced Garr to close down
the MCA mission and usher everyone over to the Apostolic Faith Mission.
Once caught in the throes of the pentecostal revival, Garr became the first
white person to speak in tongues at Azusa Street. His co-worker at the MCA
mission, Glenn Cook, was asked to take over the finances and, as a result,
contributed to the formation of an interracial leadership that guided the
early years of the revival.[60] Like the former members of the Southern California and Arizona Holiness Association who attended Azusa Street, the
Garrs, Cook and the rest of the MCA faithful were already practitioners of
sanctified unity ecclesiology before their arrival at the Apostolic Faith Mission. The little MCA mission in Los Angeles had continued the racial and
ethnic inclusiveness that was a part of the home church in Chicago.[61] Accordingly, the racial mixing that occurred during the revival created no barrier to their participation; indeed, they would have welcomed it as charac-
teristic of the New Testament church.

Charles H. Mason traveled to Los Angeles from Tennessee. A co-worker
with Charles P. Jones, the two men believed strongly in sanctified unity ecclesiology. The beginning of the revival arrived at the moment when both
men were in the midst of seeking a greater spiritual vitality for their ministries. Believing the church of the New Testament was the same "Church of
God" today, they expected the same spiritual power that was demonstrated

---

59. While the Nazarenes fervently preached the spiritual value of receiving entire
sanctification, their ecclesiology is clearly not based on sanctified unity. Carl Bangs
notes that the "new church avoided overly elaborated ecclesiasticism, but also refused to adopt the simple primitivism of the restorationist 'Church of God' movements in and out of the Holiness Movement." Carl Bangs, *Phineas F. Bresee: His Life
in Methodism, The Holiness Movement, and The Church of the Nazarene* (Kansas City,
Kans.: Beacon Hill Press of Kansas City, 1995), 202. Charles E. Jones states in reference to the Church of the Nazarene that it has "been generally apathetic toward minorities and civil rights. Between 1906 and 1936 not one Negro congregation was
reported" by them. Charles Edwin Jones, *Perfectionist Persuasion: The Holiness
Movement and American Methodism, 1867-1936* (Metuchen, N.J.: Scarecrow Press,
1974), 135.
60. See Kostlevy for a more detailed account of the events surrounding the work of
the MCA in Los Angeles. Kostlevy, "Nor Silver, Nor Gold," 235-248.
61. "Black" Susan Fogg is the best-known African-American evangelist to work with
the MCA. I want to express my thanks to William Kostlevy for drawing my attention
to Susan Fogg.

in the lives of the apostles to be evident in their own ministries. Disappointed that it was not, Mason led a group of three men to Los Angeles in 1907 to discover if the present revival could provide them what they lacked.

In their view, the restored "Church of God in Christ" not only possessed holiness and apostolic power but also broke down barriers between nationalities, races and denominations.[62] Jones worked with whites to spread the holiness message throughout Tennessee and its adjoining states. Indeed, Jones first sought out the experience of entire sanctification only after the white holiness educator Joanna P. Moore prophesied to him in 1891 that "God is going to fill you with the Holy Ghost."[63] As Dale T. Irwin notes, "like many others within the Holiness movement across the United States, Jones linked the experience of personal sanctification with the goal of realizing the unity of the church."[64] For Jones, as for Mason, the unity of the church must not lie exclusively at a corporate level—with the end of denominationalism and the restoration of the Church of God—but must also include a communal unity that cut across the lines of race and ethnicity. So the appearance of three representatives from the Church of God in Christ at the Azusa Street revival bolstered the strong support for sanctified unity ecclesiology already at work at the Apostolic Faith Mission.

The arrival of Gaston B. Cashwell to the Azusa Street revival in 1906 provided representation from the radical Holiness movement in North Carolina.[65] A member of Ambrose B. Crumpler's Pentecostal Holiness Church, holiness radicals could be found in the state going back into the early 1890s. Crumpler, a minister with the Methodist Episcopal Church, South, received entire sanctification in 1890 under the preaching of Beverly Carradine. By 1897 Crumpler and other holiness advocates had found the North Carolina Holiness Association. A year and a half later, on November 4, 1898, Crumpler, with three other Methodist ministers, founded the Pentecostal Holi-

---

62. David Daniels observes that Charles Mason was significantly influenced by William Christian, leader of an independent black restorationist movement, which disavowed "unscriptural titles of churches, such as Baptist and Methodist, and embracing the New Testament church as the model." See David Daniels, "Charles Harrison Mason: The Interracial Impulse of Early Pentecostalism," in *Portraits of a Generation: Early Pentecostal Leaders*, ed. Grant Wacker (Fayetteville, Ark.: The University of Arkansas Press, 2002), 259.

63. As quoted in Irvin, *Charles Price Jones*, 38.

64. Ibid., 39.

65. Even though Cashwell belonged to a radical holiness church that practiced sanctified unity ecclesiology, upon his arrival in Los Angeles he soon learned that he needed to experience an even deeper death to his racial prejudice. As a holiness radical he instinctively returned to the experience of sanctification to help him overcome the inappropriate racial attitudes revealed in him at Azusa Street. The story is told more completely in chapter five.

ness Church. Crumpler's revivals and church services were frequently attended by blacks. Racist critics decried his services, saying they were for "poor folks and Negroes," a church "decent folks" should not be a part of. Nonetheless, the church continued to break the social mores of the South and practice sanctified unity ecclesiology.[66]

The Pentecostal Holiness Church merged with the Fire-Baptized Holiness Church in 1911. Founded by Benjamin Hardin Irwin in the mid-1890s in Iowa, the Fire-Baptized Holiness Church rapidly spread throughout the Midwest and down into North Carolina. The F.B.H. Church also practiced sanctified unity ecclesiology. Not only were churches and conventions integrated, but the African-American leader, William E. Fuller, was placed on the executive board and given one of the four most important offices by 1905.[67]

The Azusa Street revival, from 1906 to 1909, attracted radical holiness folk from every significant hub in the country. Representatives with contacts in Southern California, Chicago, Indiana and Cincinnati, Tennessee and North Carolina all found their way to Los Angeles. Through holiness journals, revivals and word of mouth, the communication system among holiness radicals was quite efficient. That this effective means of communication drew the saints to Azusa Street demonstrates that the Los Angeles revival at its foundation was part of the radical Holiness movement. With the notable exception of the pentecostal message, most of the preaching at the revival and many of the articles printed in the *Apostolic Faith* reveal significant dependence on radical holiness theology. For these reasons it is included in this study on sanctified unity ecclesiology. It is also clear that Azusa Street became a watershed moment where holiness radicals separated over the pentecostal message. Nevertheless, the revival in Los Angeles can, in many ways, be seen as the climax of an ecclesiology that brought together Christians from across racial and ethnic lines.

It is true that sanctified unity ecclesiology continued in both radical holiness and pentecostal circles, but one senses that its influence began to wane as the Azusa Street revival came to an end. There are probably many reasons for this. First and foremost, the establishment of segregationist laws across the country continued to frustrate any effort to hold integrated revivals or establish racially inclusive and multiethnic churches. As well, the acceptance of premillennialism created an atmosphere of urgency that sacrificed efforts at integration on the altar of evangelism. Integration raised barriers between the saints' evangelistic message and their audience, so it was dropped, by whites, blacks and browns, so that the greatest number of people could be ready for the soon coming of Christ. Still, in the end, a common set of theological suppositions and working relationships sup-

---

66. For the best history of the Pentecostal Holiness Church see Vinson Synan, *The Old-Time Power* (Franklin Press, Ga.: Advocate Press, 1973), 55-81.
67. Ibid., 81-100.

porting an ecclesiology of sanctified unity among holiness radicals can be traced from the teaching of Daniel Warner's Church of God Reformation Movement to the preaching of William J. Seymour and the Azusa Street revival.

Chapter Two

Theological Background to Sanctified Unity Ecclesiology

Before proceeding to discuss the development of sanctified unity ecclesiology, it is first necessary to explore its theological background. Key theological developments took place in nineteenth-century American evangelicalism that made possible the emergence of interracial and multiethnic churches.

The first, and most important, was the development of the Wesleyan doctrine of entire sanctification. At its core, entire sanctification taught the eradication of the sin nature within each believer, which, they believed, restored the ability among sanctified Christians to express perfect love towards their neighbors. The profound nature of the experience many times caused the saints to think, and often times act, outside of the cultural and social limitations of their day.

Wesley's insight that holiness was the core of the Christian faith soon became the *sine qua non* of much of American evangelicalism. Given direct expression in the Holiness movement, holiness advocates set out to sanctify the individual, the church and society at large. This set the stage for an eventual dispute over the nature of the church and the subsequent break from the Holiness movement by holiness radicals.

The development of radical holiness eschatology contributed to the ecclesiological debate by creating a static view of the nature of the church. The church as found in the New Testament established a permanent model to be followed by all Christians in all ages. The saints considered any deviation from the biblical model to be symptomatic of the sinful influences that had worked their way into the church throughout previous centuries. This was especially true of holiness and unity as it defined the New Testament church. Furthermore, their eschatological interpretations of the biblical text led them to believe that the New Testament church, the Church of God, had been restored in their time. As a result holiness radicals concluded that denominational Christianity was now to be left behind as the holiness faithful became part of the restored Church of God.

33

This chapter will detail the saints' understanding of the doctrines of sanctification and eschatology as they gave rise to a restorationist impulse inside the radical Holiness movement. Both doctrines formed the foundation for the emergence of sanctified unity ecclesiology. Eschatological restorationism explained to the saints that their generation was indeed the end of a long historical process through which God was restoring his original church and readying his bride for his returning Son. Sanctification created the visible holiness within the church that made her worthy of being wedded to the King of Kings.[1] The two together allowed the saints to press for the complete ecclesiological unity of the saints, corporately and communally, which became the hallmark of sanctified unity ecclesiology.

Entire Sanctification

The Holiness doctrine of entire sanctification originated in the evangelical teachings of John Wesley. In his sermon "On Working Out Our Own Salvation," Wesley argued that salvation by faith consisted of both justification and sanctification.

By justification we are saved from the guilt of sin, and restored to the favour of God; by sanctification we are saved from the power and root of sin, and restored to the image of God. All experience, as well as Scripture, show this salvation to be both instantaneous and gradual. It begins the moment we are justified, in the holy, humble, gentle, patient love of God and man. It gradually increases from that moment, as a "grain of mustard-seed, which, at first, is the least of all seeds," but afterwards puts forth large branches, and becomes a great tree; till, in another instant, the heart is cleansed from all sin, and filled with pure love to God and man. But even that love increases more and more, till we "grow up in all things into Him that is our Head;" till we attain "the measure of the stature of the fullness of Christ."[2]

Wesley referred to biblical holiness as Christian Perfection. By this he did not mean to imply that sanctified Christians were exempt from sin borne in ignorance, mental mistakes or even temptation, but that they possessed the spiritual orientation to prevent a "voluntary transgression of a

---

1. "The movement for the 'deepening' of the Christian life, now extending throughout all Christendom, is the preparation of the Bride, for holiness will be her trousseau. When she has been made ready then Christ will return, catch her away in the clouds, and the following announcement will be proclaimed: 'The marriage of the Lamb has come, and his wife hath made herself ready. And to her was granted that she should be arrayed in fine linen, clean white, for the fine linen is the righteousness of saints.'" Excerpt from J. O. McClurkan's *Behold He Cometh.* See Strickland and Dunning, *J. O. McClurkan,* 124.
2. *The Works of John Wesley, Vol. 6, First Series of Sermons Continued Second Series Begun (through 86),* 4th ed. (Grand Rapids, Mich.: Zondervan, 1958), 509.

known law."[3] Wesley's strict definition of Christian Perfection guarded his theology against the charge that he taught "sinless perfection," an accusation he adamantly denied. Wesley also taught that entire sanctification enabled the believer to practice "perfect love." If one aspect of Christian Perfection involved personal holiness then, equally, it meant love of God and neighbor. As Harald Lindstrom has put it, "Positively, then, perfection is firstly perfect love. Negatively, it is perfect deliverance from sin."[4]

Wesley's determination to spread scriptural holiness throughout the land did not mean that he had ready-made answers for every theological question concerning the second grace of sanctification. One question that he wrestled with during his entire ministry entailed whether sanctification occurred at the end of life, or during an earlier period. While it is generally assumed that the obtainment of holiness was primarily teleological in his thinking, his own writings suggest that he was filled with ambivalence on the matter. In a 1767 summary appended to *A Plain Account of Christian Perfection* Wesley equivocated, "I believe this instant generally is the instant of death, the moment before the soul leaves the body. But I believe it may be ten, twenty or forty years before. I believe it is usually many years after justification; but that it may be within five years or five months after it, I know of no conclusive argument to the contrary."[5]

A second question that occupied his thinking, not unrelated to the first, pertained to the exact process of sanctification: did it happen gradually or instantaneously? William Faupel describes Wesley's position on this question as a "progressive/instantaneous dialectic."[6] In point of fact the pastoral nature of Wesley's approach to sanctification provided great latitude to the individual believer. Nevertheless, he reasoned that if "sin cease before death, there must, in the nature of the thing, be an instantaneous change, there must be a last moment wherein it does exist, and a first moment it does not."[7] Wesley's ambiguity on the point did not hold for long within Methodist circles.[8] Within the emerging nineteenth-century revival cam-

---

3. John Wesley, *A Plain Account of Christian Perfection* (London: Epworth Press, 1952), 45.

4. Harald Lindstrom, *Wesley and Sanctification: A Study in the Doctrine of Salvation* (Nappanee, Ind.: Francis Asbury Press, 1980), 130-131.

5. Wesley, *Christian Perfection*, 112.

6. Faupel, *Everlasting Gospel*, 63.

7. *The Works of John Wesley*, Vol. 8, *Addresses, Essays, Letters*, 4th ed. (Grand Rapids, Mich.: Zondervan, 1958), 329.

8. Stephen John Lennox's recent dissertation on the Holiness movement's use of Scripture agrees with this assessment. "Whether such an experience would be early in the Christian's walk with God or toward the end, whether it was accomplished instantaneously, gradually, or by some synthesis of the two, and the method by which this grace would be bestowed, these were questions about which Wesley remained ambiguous." Stephen John Lennox, "Biblical Interpretation in the Amercan Holiness Movement, 1875-1920" (Ph.D, diss., Drew University, 1992), 82.

paigns taking place on the American continent the teleological aspect of Wesley's view of sanctification quickly gave way to an early and instantaneous work of God.

The Methodist lay theologian Phoebe Palmer did much to advance the Wesleyan telos of entire sanctification to the front end of the Christian experience. A key leader in the first phase of the Holiness movement, Phoebe Palmer, along with her sister Sarah Lankford and husband Dr. Walter Palmer, started the "Tuesday Meeting for the Promotion of Holiness" where interested parties, including some of the leading bishops of the Methodist Episcopal Church, met to seek a deeper work of holiness in their lives. Casting aside all the tortured ambiguity of Wesley's thinking, Palmer contended for a "shorter way" to Christian Perfection.[9] Borne out of her own inability to experience the assurance of the "second blessing," Palmer came to believe that faith exercised in the proper pursuit of holiness was always answered by God. Her "altar theology," as it became known, spelled out the concrete steps the believer must take to acquire entire sanctification. "Mrs. Palmer believed that the Scriptures taught that Christ was both the sacrifice for her sin and the altar upon which she could offer up her whole heart in consecration to God."[10]

"On everyone who will specifically present himself upon the altar . . . for the sole object of being ceaselessly consumed, body and soul in the self-sacrificing service of God, He will cause the fire to descend. And . . . he will not delay to do this for every waiting soul, for He standeth waiting, and the moment the offerer presents the sacrifice, the hallowing, consuming touch will be given."[11]

Not only did Palmer develop a repeatable procedure for the church to administer, but she also argued for the immediacy of the experience. Soon the pursuit of holiness among Christians of every denominational stripe would be wedded to the presentism of American revivalism. Palmer's "altar theology" became the stock and trade of holiness evangelists across the United States. As holiness preachers directed their hearers to the necessity of the "double cure" they never tired of waxing eloquent on its profound benefits.

For other perspectives on Wesley's understanding of entire sanctification see Jones, *Perfectionist Persuasion*, 4; Dieter, *Holiness Revival*, 31; Timothy L. Smith, "The Holiness Crusade," in *History of American Methodism*, ed. Emory S. Bucke, vol. 2 (New York: Abingdon, 1964), 608-627; John L. Peters, *Christian Perfection and American Methodism* (Grand Rapids: Francis Asbury-Zondervan, 1985 [1956]), 31, 48, 57.

9. "Wesley produced a generation of seekers after holiness, Palmer produced holiness professors." See Lennox, "Biblical Interpretation," 91.

10. Dieter, *The Holiness Revival*, 23.

11. As quoted in Dieter, *The Holiness Revival*, 24.

Experiencing Holiness

You can't think of a Holy God

Sitting in a HOLY HEAVen

Surrounded by HOLY Angels

Giving out a HOLY LAW

Sending out a HOLY SON

To provide a HOLY redemption

By his HOLY BLOOD

And instituted a HOLY CHURCH

With HOLY HYMNS

And HOLY SACraments

And HOLY COVenants

And sent his HOLY SPIRIT

Into the world to

EFFECT that very purpose,

You can't think of THAT God

Expecting LESS of us

Than holiness.[12]

No point of doctrine was of more importance to the saints than holiness. Holiness provided the starting point through which every other doctrine was interpreted. The experience and life of holiness allowed sanctified Christians to express their faith in new and surprising ways. For example, it was remarkable how many saints testified that soon after experiencing the "second blessing"[13] they acquired an unexpected ability to write and sing original songs.[14] To those inside the movement the life of holiness was

---

12. J. Lawrence Brasher, *The Sanctified South: John Larkin Brasher and the Holiness Movement* (Urbana: University of Illinois Press, 1994), 113. The above sermon was taken from a recording of John Larkin Brasher preaching. Voice inflections were provided by J. Lawrence Brasher.

13. Vinson Synan notes that the "second blessing," or "entire sanctification," was "also called 'holiness,' 'a pure heart,' 'perfect love,' 'moving into Canaan,' 'the double cure,' and 'the Baptism with the Holy Spirit." See Synan, *The Old-Time Power*, 58.

14. Daniel Warner, founder and leader of the Church of God Reformation Movement, Martin Wells Knapp, radical holiness evangelist from Cincinnati, and Charles Price Jones, founder of the Church of Christ (Holiness) U.S.A., are three examples of indi-

filled with a sweet joy. One African-American woman of the Southern California and Arizona Holiness Association explained that the "Book of Rules and Regulations all seemed right to me. I love the way of Holiness. It does not seem a hard way for me, but glorious High-way."[15] But what was it about the experience of entire sanctification that created such new possibilities for spiritual growth? And how did one receive the "second blessing?"

The simplicity and logic of entire sanctification attracted many to the holiness message. Holiness adherents preached that the spiritual premise underlying the need for the "double cure" was found in Heb 12:14: "Follow peace with all men, and holiness, without which no man shall see the Lord." The Bible, they taught, called for holiness as a necessary condition to enter heaven. "Do you think anything that has *'the nature of sin in it'* can get into heaven? The pearly gates are closed against you, until you get rid of this infection of nature that has the every essence of sin in it (emphasis his)," exclaimed the Reverend A. M. Hills.[16] But if this seemed daunting to some it was not to the advocates of holiness. Indeed, it was a "spiritual experience divinely and freely provided for everyone" from the beginning of the Christian era to the present.[17] Or as early Church of God Reformation Movement historian A. L. Byers wrote, the "doctrine was nothing more or less than one of the great Scriptural truths that has been obscured by the apostasy."[18]

In the main, advocates of entire sanctification followed the teaching of Phoebe Palmer's "altar theology." In Heb 13:10 Jesus is referenced as the altar. Sanctified teaching then combined Heb 13:10 with Matt 23:19 to declare that since Jesus is the altar it is the altar which sanctifies. It was his great sacrifice on the cross that prepared the altar as a place where the justified believer received sanctification. Heb 13:2 states, "Wherefore Jesus also, that he might SANCTIFY the people with his own blood suffered without the gate."[19] Then, following Rom 12:1, 2, the believer placed him or herself on the altar as a "living sacrifice" to receive the experience through faith. C. A. McCoy of Dimenin, Iowa, described it this way, "I learned it would take faith in the blood of Jesus to cleanse this depravity away, so ac-

---

viduals who experienced a new and prolific ability to write and publish Christian hymns after receiving entire sanctification.

15. Washburn, History and Reminiscences, 169.

16. Reverend A. M. Hills, *The Cleansing Baptism* (Manchester: Star Hall, 1908), 16.

17. L. Howard Juillerat, *Brief History of the Church of God* (Cleveland, Tenn.: Church of God Publishing House, 1922), 21.

18. A. L. Byers, *Birth of a Reformation: Or The Life and Labors of Daniel S. Warner* (Anderson, Ind.: Gospel Trumpet Company, 1921), 113. The Church of God Reformation Movement, like other Believer churches, believed that the church "fell into apostasy" with the ascendancy of the Roman Catholic Church.

19. An unsigned article in *The Revivalist* arguing for the experience of entire sanctification put the word "sanctify" in complete capital letters to stress the important connection between sanctification and the blood of Jesus. "The Blood," *The Revivalist* (Cincinnati, Ohio) 7, no. 12 (December 1893): 2.

cording to Rom 12: 1-2, I made a living sacrifice."[20] The result in accordance with 1 Thess 5:22, 23 meant the believer was now wholly sanctified.[21]

Conforming to the ethos of frontier revivalism, the believer became "a living sacrifice" through his own individual decision to place himself on the altar. Nonbelievers could not experience the second grace of sanctification at the time of justification since "a sinner, being dead in trespasses and sins, Eph 2:1, could not present a *living* sacrifice (emphasis his)."[22] Rather it was available only for the regenerated person who was now in the spiritual po-

---

20. Washburn, History and Reminiscences, 178-179.

21. Radical holiness teaching was uniform on this matter as evidenced by the following sample of explanations taken from radical holiness groups across the United States. Martin Wells Knapp summarized the entire process: "the altar here mentioned is Jesus Christ [Heb. 10: 12]. As the victim He died; as the priest He offered Himself, and His divine nature was the altar upon which the sacrifice was made. The Savior then is the Christian's altar. Upon Him I lay myself. The altar sanctifies the gift. The blood cleanses from all sin, personal and inbred. . . . The instant we add a perfect faith to a perfect consecration the work is done and the blessing descends. . . ." Martin Wells Knapp, *Double Cure* (Cincinnati, Ohio: God's Revivalist Office, 1898), 77. James F. Washburn condensed the experience to one sentence, "Hundreds all over the land are testifying that the great Altar, Jesus, sanctifies their gift and that the blood of Jesus cleanseth from all sin and that the very God of peace does sanctify them wholly as expressed in Paul's prayer, 1 Thess. 5: 23." James F. Washburn, "You May Be Sanctified," *Pentecost* (Los Angeles) 1, no. 8 (March 27, 1886): 7. Mrs. Leah E. Sheets, a lay person in the Fire-Baptized Holiness Church, gave a personal description. "I then sought a clean heart, to be sanctified wholly, and on the night of June 5, 1895, I presented my body a living sacrifice, holy, acceptable, which was my reasonable service, I had consecrated all to God, home and surroundings, friends, parents, brother and sister, husband and child, time, talent and earthly store, then my body, a living sacrifice, on the altar, Jesus. He sanctified the gift. I died. He cleansed out the carnal nature-the old man with all his deeds." Mrs. Leah E. Sheets, "Experience and Testimony of Mrs. Leah E. Sheets," *Live Coals of Fire* (Lincoln, Nebraska) 1, no. 1 (October 6, 1899): 6. Church historian David Daniels notes that African-American holiness evangelist, Charles Price Jones, "used the altar imagery of Romans 12:1 as Phoebe Palmer and others did as well as the baptismal imagery of Pentecost. He highlighted the cleansing and washing themes associated with the baptismal imagery. . . . Using altar phraseology, he spoke of believers being 'on the altar sacrificed' because 'sin and self we denied.'" David Daniels, "The Cultural Renewal of Slave Religion: Charles Price Jones and the Emergence of the Holiness Movement" (Ph.D, diss., Union Theological Seminary, 1992), 145. Finally, J. O. McClurkan espouses a similar version of Palmer's "altar theology" in his book *How to Keep Sanctified*. "The Bible says that the altar sanctifies the gift—Matt. 23:19, that it maketh everything holy that toucheth it—Ex. 29:37. Christ is your altar. You have laid it all on him, and his blood cleanses you from all sin—1 John 1:7. When your faith appropriated these promises he sanctified you." Strickland and Dunning, *J. O. McClurkan*, 108.

22. George M. Teel, *The New Testament Church* (Los Angeles, Ca: Pentecost Printing House, 1901), 118.

sition to offer himself to God for sanctification. Many sought entire sanctification the moment after they came into saving faith. For others it took years to admit the need for the purifying effects of holiness doctrine. Seth Rees admitted that for him he "reached a state of conviction, even after I had preached for years, when the wretchedness and anguish of my heart was often inconceivable. My suffering under conviction for inbred sin greatly surpassed anything I endured when an awakened sinner."[23] Benjamin Irwin described the basis of a believer's decision to seek entire sanctification this way: "We go down before God, having had a revelation from God of the inbred sin of our hearts and having seen the turpitude and vileness of inherent depravity, and realizing that God has promised to wash us in His blood...."[24]

A key component of the theology of entire sanctification in the thinking of holiness folk was the idea of Jesus' blood, and its relationship to the Holy Spirit. The efficacious nature of the blood of Jesus extended beyond the evangelical message of justification to include sanctification. The connection between the blood of Christ and holiness rested on three key verses: 1 John 1:7, Heb 10:19 and Heb 13:2.[25] Together these verses elaborated the role of the blood in holiness theology: it cleansed believers of all sin through sanctification so that the saint might prove capable of approaching a holy God. As George M. Teel exalted in his book *The New Testament Church*, "Jesus shed His blood to sanctify the people . . . What a glorious thought! Jesus shed His blood to sanctify us."[26] For holiness advocates the purifying power of the blood was the crux of the sanctifying process. As a result, this theological approach is ubiquitous in the preaching and writings of the saints. Beverly Carradine is representative of the intense connection sanctified preachers observed between holiness and the blood of Jesus:

> The Bible does not say that the blood and something else cleanseth, but *The Blood!* So, if the world to-day would renounce its beads, pilgrimages, and works of righteousness, and look to the blood of Christ, it would be saved. If Christians would turn their gaze from the thought of growth, development and church work to the purifying blood of Jesus, the heart purity or holiness they desire would be instantly given (emphasis his).[27]

---

23. Seth Rees, *The Ideal Pentecostal Church* (Cincinnati, Ohio: M. W. Knapp, 1899), 84.

24. Benjamin Irwin, "A Whirlwind from the North, Part 1," *Live Coals of Fire* (Lincoln, Nebraska) 1, no. 7 (December 1, 1899): 3.

25. "But if we walk in the light, as he is in the light, we have fellowship one with another, and the Blood of Jesus Christ his Son cleanseth us from all sin," 1 John 1:7; "Having therefore, brethren, boldness to enter into the holiest by the blood of Jesus," Heb 10:19; "Wherefore Jesus also, that he might sanctify the people with his own blood suffered without the gate," Heb 13:2.

26. Teel, *The New Testament Church*, 99.

George L. Cole clearly believed that the blood of Jesus was the corrective for generational sin:

> Time will not purge this old leaven of malice out. Nothing but the blood of Jesus will sweep it away. Let us cry, The Blood, the blood, and preach the blood, and demand all to get under the blood of Jesus until redeemed from the vain conversation learned from the traditions of their fathers.[28]

As one writer in *The Revivalist* eloquently put it, "The stain of sin is so deep that no chemical but the Blood can cleanse it. Its disease so stubborn that no other remedy can cure it."[29]

When Jane Williams, African-American evangelist for the Church of God Reformation Movement, wrote Daniel Warner seeking help in carrying the "full gospel" to the people of Augusta, Georgia, she noted the lack of sanctified workers on hand with a reference to the blood of Jesus. "The Lord has a few blood washed ones here, and we long to see your faces in the flesh, so you could more fully establish the little Church of God at this place, in the true faith of the Gospel."[30] George Goings made the same plea for help in a letter published in *The Pentecost* when he noted that "while we ask God to send a thousand more blood-washed men and women to carry the full gospel to the poor dusky heathen of Africa, but let us remember that behind us are 7 ½ millions of African descent who know but little or nothing of the full gospel."[31]

The second half of the nineteenth century witnessed the rise in the use of pentecostal language to explain the benefits of sanctification within the radical Holiness movement. As the language of empowerment joined the traditional Wesleyan verbiage as a way of expressing the "second blessing," the experience took on two distinct aspects. First, the traditional Methodist approach holding that the sin nature was eradicated by the blood of Jesus continued to be seen as fundamental to victorious Christian living. But in addition to this result another was added that emphasized the empowerment the Christian received in entire sanctification. The eradication of the sin nature through the blood became a prerequisite to the reception of power from the Spirit. Martin Wells Knapp exhorted the faithful that "THIS VERY MOMENT the Fountain is open, the blood is efficacious to cleanse, and the Spirit mighty to endue with power."[32] Similarly, George M. Teel argued,

---

27. Beverly Carradine, *The Sanctified Life* (Cincinnati, Ohio: M. W. Knapp, 1890), 75-76.

28. George L. Cole, "National Prejudice," *Gospel Trumpet* (Moundsville, W. Va.) 18, no. 48 (December 1, 1898): 1.

29. "The Blood," *The Revivalist* (Cincinnati, Ohio) 7, no. 12 (December 1893): 2.

30. Smith, *Holiness and Unity*, 163.

31. George A. Goings, "How Shall We Reach Them?" *The Pentecost* (Los Angeles) 13th year, no. 263 (March 26, 1897): 30.

So we see the general marks of sanctification are, the old man crucified, the soul filled with the Holy Ghost-all baptized into *one body* by *one* Spirit. This is all done in a moment. All the sanctified souls in this world are necessarily *one*, in the sense of being purified by faith in the Blood of Jesus and being filled with love (emphasis his).[33]

Finally, Benjamin Irwin, founder and leader of the Fire-Baptized Holiness Church, also drew important distinctions between the blood of Jesus and work of the Spirit. Irwin's distinctions are important for they foreshadow the differentiation that the saints at the Azusa Street revival made with the advent of the Pentecostal movement. Believing that there was a grace to be received subsequent to entire sanctification, what he called "the fire," Irwin was sure to note the differing roles for the work of the blood and the work of the Spirit. "It is not the fire that cleanses from sin; it is the blood that does this. The blood, the blood, is all my plea. Hallelujah, it cleanses me."[34]

Not every explicator of entire sanctification made the distinction between eradication and empowerment as clearly as Knapp, Teel and Irwin. Sometimes the terms of entire sanctification and the baptism of the Holy Spirit were used interchangeably without much confusion on the part of the reader or listener. But what must be kept clear to understand the significance of entire sanctification within radical holiness theology, including the Azusa Street revival, is that the blood of Jesus was a common way of referencing the experience of the "second blessing."

To buttress the theology of entire sanctification, holiness preachers enlisted the lives of the disciples as prime examples of the qualitative difference in the spiritual condition of the justified and sanctified Christian. Martin Wells Knapp put the point best in a January, 1893 article in *The Revivalist*:

That he [Peter] and all the other Apostles except Judas, whom Jesus Himself declared to be the "son of perdition," were truly converted before Pentecost, is seen from the following facts: *Their names were written in heaven . . . . They preached by the authority of Jesus . . . . Jesus declared them to be the branches of which He was the vine . . . . They "forsook all" and followed Christ . . . . Though converted they were not yet fully Sanctified . . . . They were unstable . . . . They were self-seeking . . . . They were rash . . . . They were fearful . . . .* They were encouraged to believe that a better experience awaited them. They had repeated promises that they should be "purified," "filled" and endued with power from on high.[35]

---

32. Knapp, *Christ Crowned Within* (Saratoga Springs, N.Y.: Marion Tract Depository, 1898), 185.

33. George M. Teel, "The Oneness," *The Pentecost* (Los Angeles) 1, no. 15 (November 13, 1886): 8.

34. Benjamin H. Irwin, "A Whirlwind from the North, Part 1," *Live Coals of Fire* (Lincoln, Nebraska) 1, no. 7 (December 1, 1899): 3.

The constitutional difference between the two states was evident in the role of the self in the life of the believer. Reverend Beverly Carradine argued in his book *The Sanctified Life* that it "is well to remember that a new heart is one thing, and pure heart another. They are not synonymous. A man can have a new heart which loves God, and yet not possess a pure heart from which self, man-fear, love of praise and other like things are banished."[36]

As might be expected, different Christians had different reactions to the experience. J. Lawrence Brasher discovered that his experience of sanctification in 1900 transformed his entire ministry. He judged that his "old sermons weren't worth a nickel. . . . I had to start new as if I'd never been a preacher." The changes in his preaching were so dramatic it seemed "I began to speak in a new tongue."[37] In a similar vein, Brasher noted that fellow evangelist Bud Robinson trumpeted that during his "baptism" God "wasted grace enough on him to save the state of Texas." Brasher's wife Minnie, in contrast, experienced a "quiet peace."[38] An article entitled "A Ladder From Guilt to Glory" appearing in 1893 in *The Revivalist* expressed the divine qualities experienced by the sanctified Christian, "The air they breathe is wafted from heavenly realms, and is redolent with celestial fragrance. They know now what it is not only to have joy but 'joy unspeakable and full of glory.'"[39] To give yet one more example of the exalted state that the saints entered into during sanctification, Seth Rees recalled,

> At last there began to creep into my soul a tranquil feeling, a holy hush, a death to stillness, a sweet, placid "second rest." . . . "The old man" was "put off," "the body of sin" was "destroyed," "the old leaven" was "purged out,"

---

35. Martin Wells Knapp, "Before and After the Revival," *The Revivalist* (Cincinnati, Ohio) 7, no. 1 (January 1893): 1.

36. Carradine, *Sanctified Life*, 5-6.

37. Brasher, *The Sanctified South*, 63.

38. Ibid., 140.

39. "A Ladder from Guilt to Glory," *The Revivalist* (Cincinnati, Ohio) 7, no. 3 (March 1893): 4. A poem that relates similar sentiments was published by Oville L. Snow, "My Experience," *The Pentecost* (Los Angeles) 1, no. 7 (February 26, 1886): 7.
The carnal mind He too destroyed,
The prone the other way,
And in its place his Spirit gave;
    And gladly I obey,
I'm walking now in Beulah's clime
    Ethereal world I'm in-
Where air is fragrant with God's breath
Molested not by sin.
My brow is circled with a crown,
    My eye beholds the King'
My spirit soars in freedoms air,
And round me angels sing.

"the flesh" was "cut away," "the son of the bondwoman" was "excommuni-cated," "the carnal mind" was "crucified," and I was dead indeed unto sin.[40]

Besides the spiritual intensity that usually accompanied the experience of entire sanctification, what was most dramatic about the "second bless-ing", and most emphasized by radical holiness preachers, was the belief that the "sinful nature" had been removed completely and instantaneously. Seth Rees, known as the "Earth-Quaker" for his powerful preaching and connec-tion to The Society of Friends, articulated well the revolutionary nature of "second blessing" theology:

> The Pentecostal power, the power of the Holy Ghost, lays an axe at the very root of the tree, and, instead of dealing with branches and limbs, it attacks and destroys all roots of pride, anger, jealousy, malice, envy, strife, impa-tience, worldliness, unholy ambition, lust, and all impurity even in its most complex ramifications.[41]

Radical holiness doctrine held that the effects of the "fall" on man's na-ture were eradicated through the sanctifying altar of Christ. Daniel Warner stated that "Perfection as applied to redeemed souls, denotes the complete moral restoration of man from the effects of the fall."[42] In other words, with the application of the "double cure" the believer was morally restored to the pristine days of the Garden of Eden.[43] With the removal of the carnal na-ture holiness folk believed that they had recovered the complete image of God. The image of God in man was found in his holiness. Hence, once holi-ness was restored then the image of God was likewise reestablished.

"I teach that we were originally created holy, in the likeness of God, with all appetites normal in strength. Satan spoiled our likeness to God by inject-ing carnality, depravity into human beings. The baptism with the Holy Spir-it brings us back again to the lost image of God, and makes us normal be-ings, minus that pent-up evil, the carnality that is enmity against God."[44]

The eradication of the carnal nature, that which created the propensity towards sin in the life of the justified believer, also meant new possibilities for Christian living. Now the sanctified Christian could follow Christ with confidence that the very inclination of his nature was towards what was holy. "The last iota of evil is purged out of his nature and he is inclined only

---

40. Seth Rees, *The Ideal Pentecostal Church*, 85.

41. Ibid., 22.

42. As quoted in Barry L. Callen, *Contours of a Cause: The Theological Vision of the Church of God Movement (Anderson)* (Anderson, Ind.: Old Paths Tract Society, 1995), 144.

43. ". . . if therefore there is a restoration to be received subsequently to regenera-tion, it must consist of a cleansing from inbred depravity, which would be a restora-tion to the state of purity from which Adam fell in the garden of Eden." See William G. Schell, *The Better Testament; or, The Two Testaments Compared* (Moundsville, W.Va.: Gospel Trumpet Publishing Company, 1899), 199.

44. Hills, *Cleansing Baptism*, 45-46.

to good, and to do right is as natural to him as it was to sin while in the sinful state."[45] W. B. Godbey put it starkly in his 1884 book *Sanctification*, "A venerable saint said to me a few days ago: 'Brother Godbey, have not all Christians besetting sins?' 'No, brother, sanctified Christians have no besetting sins."[46]

The benefits of entire sanctification did not end with the removal of the sin nature, but had significant ramifications for the church's ecclesiology. Employing traditional Wesleyan language, the saints taught that the Christian could now begin to grow in perfect love towards others.[47] Secondly, the "double cure" enabled holiness folk "to serve God in holiness and righteousness all the days of this life."[48] Finally, sanctified Christians discovered that their ministries manifested a new spiritual vitality that overshadowed their previous experience. Martin Wells Knapp's aptly entitled book *Lightening Bolts* dynamically portrayed how the new work of God reoriented the lives of the saints: "this baptism transforms weaklings into giants, imparts all needed power to effectively witness, work, pray, preach, give, endure, deny, suffer, sing, write, shout, vote, or die for God as He may will."[49]

The radical Holiness movement also adhered to Wesley's views on the limitations of sanctification. Daniel Warner wrote that holiness should not be construed to mean a complete "physical, or mental restoration, for that will not be until the resurrection."[50] Knapp made a similar point, "it does not exempt from mistakes, 'sins of ignorance,' but from inbred sin and sinning against light."[51] And in another place he wrote that it "was not a work which exempted from infirmities, temptation, danger of falling, or mistakes."[52] Christian perfection redesigned the heart so that holiness could be lived out in the present. It did not apply to the mind or attributes associated with thinking. "Sanctification does not give us perfect judgment," George

---

45. Schell, *Better Testament*, 310.

46. Reverend W. B. Godbey, *Sanctification* (Dallas: Holiness Echoes, 1956 [first printing, 1884]), 56.

47. For example, Martin Wells Knapp taught that after sanctification the Christian was ready to move "out on the great ocean of perfect love," or after being delivered from the Egypt of sin was put "in possession of the Canaan of perfect love." See Martin Wells Knapp, "Lesson by the Way," *The Revivalist* (Cincinnati, Ohio) 11, no. 31 (August 3, 1899): 15; Martin Wells Knapp, "Entire Sanctification," *The Revivalist* 12, no. 12 (March 22, 1900): 3. Chapter three will explore more fully the impact of entire sanctification on radical holiness ecclesiology.

48. "Christian Perfection," *The Burning Bush*, (October 20, 1904): 15.

49. Knapp, *Lightening Bolts from Pentecostal Skies or Devices of the Devil Unmasked* (Cincinnati, Ohio: Office of the Revivalist, 1898), 17.

50. Callen, *Contours of a Cause*, 144.

51. Martin W. Knapp, "Entire Sanctification," *The Revivalist* 12, no. 12 (March 22, 1900): 3.

52. Knapp, *Lightening Bolts*, 35.

M. Teel, future president of the Southern California and Arizona Holiness Association wrote to *The Pentecost* in 1886.[53] Facing the same criticisms that Wesley did in his day, radical holiness preachers felt the need to explain quite often that they were not preaching "sinless perfection."[54] Entire sanctification removed the propensity to sin, not the possibility of it. Reverend B. Carradine believed the confusion rested with the critics of holiness. "Is it not surprising that they can not see the difference between the evil inclination and liability to sin? The power to sin is one thing, the proneness to do so is another. Sanctification takes out the latter, but leaves the former. . . ."[55]

Radical holiness teaching affirmed that the state of sanctification could be lost as well. William G. Schell admonished the faithful of the Church of God Reformation Movement to maintain their holiness through obedience to the Word of God.[56] In *The Ideal Pentecostal Church*, Seth Rees accepted the possibility of the sanctified believer backsliding after the experience. But it need not be that way, he argued, for "certainly it is not necessary to sin." He continued, "We are not preaching impeccability, but we are magnifying the grace of God in its ability and power to save from sin and make the human heart victorious."[57] Seth Rees' victorious human heart revealed an eschatological restorationist perspective which derived from his understanding of the second grace of sanctification. God's grace had become available in the last days as it had been in the time of the early church, and yet the restored "Church of God" believed an unprecedented eschatological outpouring of God's Spirit and power was taking place in their midst.

Restorationism

Holiness radicals believed that God was restoring to the church of their day the original design and function of the New Testament church. The saints taught that with the rise of the Roman Catholic Church the "Church of God" entered into a period of decline that persisted until the opening salvos of the Protestant Reformation. They argued that the start of the Protestant Reformation initiated the process in God's salvation history to reconstitute the apostolic church. The restoration of the Bible to its proper place of authority, and subsequent rediscovery of key doctrines dealing with justification and later, sanctification, revealed the work of God's *heilsgeschichte*. Followers of the holiness message, however, believed that Luther, Wesley and others had stopped short of completing the restoration of God's church

---

53. Teel, "The Oneness," *Pentecost*, 8.
54. Ambrose B. Crumpler, founder of The Pentecostal Holiness Church in North Carolina, is a notable exception. See Synan, *Old-Time Power*, 56.
55. Carradine, *The Sanctified Life*, 41.
56. Schell, *The Better Testament*, 296.
57. Rees, *The Ideal Pentecostal Church*, 17.

by ignoring the essential doctrine of ecclesiology. The Protestant adherence to "human confessions" caused division among Christians which contradicted God's plan for a united church. The most important book to address the ecclesiological issues fomenting within radical Holiness circles, the *Divine Church*, written by John Brooks in 1891, stated the problem thus:

> Luther, Calvin, Wesley, and others did grand work in uncovering the wickedness of Rome, and insisting on a return to the word of God; but they all failed in making practical what they accepted as true in theory. All of them received human confessions of faith as bonds [tests] of fellowship, thus imitating the bad example which caused division in the beginning. They attempted to *reform* the Church, whereas they should have sought to restore it to its original condition of unity [emphasis his].[58]

The final restoration of the church, then, was intricately connected to its unity; and the cause of disunity resided in the lack of holiness evident in Protestant churches.

Protestant churches taught that there were two aspects to the church. First, the church that gathered on the Lord's day to worship was understood as the "visible church."

But tucked away inside the "visible church" was the "invisible church." The "invisible church" included only those who were regenerate. The mixing of regenerate and unregenerate within the same congregation caused the advocates of entire sanctification to conclude that Protestant churches lacked genuine holiness. It was this lack of holiness, the saints argued, that caused the sectarian divisions within Protestantism. Sanctified Christians believed that the theology of the "invisible" and the "visible" church was detrimental to the biblical injunction to be one. Accordingly, they pressed for the true church, the *ecclesia*, to come out and make the "invisible," "visible." Only a holy church comprised of sanctified Christians could overcome the divisiveness that is inherent in the unsanctified heart. Writing in *The Pentecost* in 1904 Alice J. Whiting stated this general sentiment among holiness folk:

> Well, then, Christ having a holy spiritual body needs a holy body of flesh to manifest this to the world. The spiritual church being holy, the visible church ought to be likewise a holy church. Every member of the spiritual being holy, every member of the visible church should be sanctified also; and God has never authorized anything else.[59]

---

58. John Brooks, *Divine Church* (New York and London: Garland, 1984 (first printing, 1891), 265.

59. Alice J. Whiting, "Why a Holy Church," *The Pentecost* (Los Angeles) 20th Year, no. 457 (December 22, 1904): 1.

Following the same line of argument, William Schell placed the stress on "visible unity" over "invisible unity."[60] In the words of Melvin Dieter the radical holiness argument resulted in the demand "that one's sect be placed on the 'altar' of consecration."[61] Thus, the restoration of New Testament ecclesiology, and its implied unity, would ensue from the sanctification of the body of Christ.

Two separate approaches to eschatology within the radical Holiness movement contributed to the saints' understanding of the restoration of the church. One popular eschatological view, known as the "evening light," developed out of the Church of God Reformation Movement. A second eschatological conviction, referred to as the "latter rain," was equally popular among many other sanctified Christians. Both approaches argued that in God's providence the church at the end of history would be the restoration of the first church. Here James W. McClendon, Jr.'s theological work on the Radical Reformation is helpful in understanding the restorationist views of the saints. He postulates that with the "reestablishment" of Scripture as the sole authority in the Christian life a link was made "between the church of the apostles and our own."[62] Furthermore, McClendon notes, this "can be expressed as a hermeneutical motto, which is shared awareness of *the present Christian community as the primitive community and the eschatological community*. In other words, the church now is the primitive church and the church on the day of judgment is the church now (emphasis his)."[63] The "evening light" and "latter rain" eschatologies, then, reinforced the radical holiness reading of history, which viewed the advent of the Protestant Reformation as the first step towards the recovering of right doctrine, ecclesiology and practice of the New Testament church.[64]

In 1895 Daniel Warner opened his article on the subject of the "evening light" with the question, "What does it mean?"[65] For adherents to the Church of God Reformation Movement the question was of paramount im-

---

60. Schell, *Is the Negro a Beast?* (Moundsville, W.Va.: Gospel Trumpet Publishing Company, 1901), 313.

61. Dieter, "Primitivism in the American Holiness Tradition," 84. The radical holiness use of the word "sect" should be understood as a reference to denominations. "Sect" was not used in the sociological sense of Ernst Troeltsch.

62. James W. McClendon, Jr., *Systematic Theology: Ethics*, (Nashville, Tenn.: Abingdon, 1986), 31. I want to express thanks to Merle Strege for directing me to McClendon's theological writings.

63. Ibid., 31.

64. John E. Stanley contends that "since its inception in 1880-1881, the ecclesiology of the Church of God, its doctrine and experience of the church, has determined its eschatology." See John E. Stanley, "Unity Amid Diversity: Interpreting The Book Of Revelation in The Church of God (Anderson)," *Wesleyan Theological Journal* 25, no. 2 (Fall 1990): 74.

65. Daniel Warner, "The Evening Light," *Gospel Trumpet* (Grand Junction, Michigan) 15 no. 29 (July 25, 1895): 1.

portance. They believed they were living in the time of the "evening light." "Evening light" eschatology was based on the scriptural passage in Zech 14:6, 7, which stated, "And it shall come to pass in that day, that the light shall not be clear, nor dark: but it shall one day which shall be known to the Lord, not day, nor night: but it shall come to pass, that at evening time it shall be light." The Zechariah passage became the interpretive key for Warner and the "evening light" saints, as they became known.

Citing Isa 58:5, John 8:56 and 2 Cor 6:2, Warner postulated that the "entire dispensation of Christ is called a day."[66] He reasoned that every day has a morning and evening. Moreover, since Jesus is the light of the world, the beginning of Christianity represented the morning light of the present dispensational day. Looking to the scriptures for a description of the first followers of Christ, Warner found that they consisted of "an holy nation" formed in "one body" and called the "Church of God."

With the ascendancy of the Roman Catholic Church, the Church of God fell into the dark night of human organization. The Roman Catholic Church was the first of two beasts spoken of in Revelation 13. The apostasy lasted for 1260 years. Perfect light was not restored at the end of the apostasy; rather, as Zechariah noted, a new era began that was "not day, nor night." This was the Protestant church, the second beast. Warner's exegesis argued that the restoration of the gospel message during the Protestant Reformation was part of the morning light, but that the sectarian nature of Protestantism demonstrated that it was still enslaved to the night. Writing in the *Gospel Trumpet*, Lillie Thurmond described the problem for the Protestants this way, "they were yoked up in sectism with unbelievers, and did not see that we must live a holy life."[67] The result was a "mixture of day and night."[68]

In the year 1880 the "evening light" of the dispensational day broke forth in Warner's reconstituted Church of God Reformation Movement.[69] Citing Isa 58:8, "Then shall thy light break forth as the morning," Warner believed that the Church of God, the "evening light," was the same Church of God birthed in the "morning light" of the New Testament era. And what were to be the characteristics of the "evening light" church, the "same holiness, unity, power and gifts that shone out in the divine church in the morn-

---

66. Ibid., 1.

67. Lillie Thurmond, "Christian Unity," *Gospel Trumpet* (Moundsville, W.Va.) 18, no. 33 (August 18, 1898): 1.

68. Warner, "Evening Light," 1.

69. "It was known that Jerusalem was restored in 420 B.C. Daniel 8:14 predicts the sanctuary would be cleansed in 'two thousand and three hundred days. . . .'" Warner asserted that Daniel's 2,300 days meant 2,300 years, and pointed out that 2,300 years after 420 B.C. was A.D. 1880, the very year in which the Church of God Movement was purported to have begun." See Val Clear, *Where the Saints Have Trod: A Social History of the Church of God Reformation Movement* (Chesterfield, Ind.: Midwest Publications, 1977), 44.

ing of her dispensation on earth."[70] Their experience out in the field confirmed the saints' biblical interpretation of the "evening light." Nancy Pell wrote in from Mill, South Carolina in 1894 that "The Evening Light is truly shining here, and all true Christians are coming out."[71]

"Evening light" eschatology also influenced the thinking of A. J. Tomlinson, leader of the Church of God (Cleveland, Tennessee). The band of sanctified Christians located in the hills of Tennessee and North Carolina had originally called themselves the "Christian Union" and then the "Holiness Church," to denote their strong commitment to unity and holiness. But when Tomlinson decided to join the group in 1903 he brought with him a revelation of the one, true church, "that it is the Church of God of the Bible."[72] As historian Joseph E. Campbell summarized the events of 1903, "Their attitude was that the body of Christ should maintain the ideal of Christian union and proclaim the doctrine of holiness – but its name should be Church of God."[73]

Tomlinson's vision of the "Church of God" was grounded in "evening light" eschatology. He wrote, for instance, that the New Testament Church had "shined forth with radiant glory in the early morning of the Gospel day."[74] And then after a period of bondage, first under the Roman Catholics and then the Protestants, the apostolic church had been restored in their day since the "evening light, the true light is now shining, and the sheep are hearing His voice and are coming from every place where they have been scattered during the cloudy and dark day."[75] Tomlinson's indebtedness to the Church of God Reformation Movement's restorationist eschatology is made evident in his breakdown of God's *heilsgeschichte* into four periods: early church (morning light), Roman Catholicism (dark day), Protestantism (cloudy day) and the Church of God (evening light). He taught that the church at the end would be the same church as at the beginning. As a result, the Church of God should "expect nothing less in glory and power in the evening light than that which broke out over the eastern hills in the early morning of the gospel age."[76] Finally, Tomlinson linked "evening light" es-

---

70. Warner, "Evening Light," 1.

71. Nancy Pell, "News from the Field," *Gospel Trumpet* (Grand Junction, Michigan) 14, no. 30 (August 2, 1894): 4.

72. As quoted in Synan, *Holiness-Pentecostal Tradition*, 75.

73. Joseph E. Campbell, *The Pentecostal Holiness Church 1898-1948* (Franklin Springs, Ga.: Publishing House of the Pentecostal Holiness Church, 1951), 74. See R. G. Robins, *A. J. Tomlinson: Plainfolk Modernist* (Oxford: Oxford University Press, 2004), 183, 204.

74. Synan, *Holiness-Pentecostal Tradition*, 76

75. Ibid., 76.

76. As quoted in Grant Wacker, "The Functions of Faith in Primitive Pentecostalism," *Harvard Theological Review* 77 (July/October 1984): 365.

chatology to the restored "Church of God" in 1910 when he named the new church periodical the *Evening Light and Church of God Evangel.*[77]

Another eschatological vision which shaped the saints' perception of their own ecclesiology was the theology of the "latter rain." Radical holiness preacher George D. Watson believed that the "holiness movement is emphatically the latter rain of the outpoured Holy Spirit, which is designed to call forth the elect from the nominal believers, and to rapidly transform and ripen them for the harvest of the coming of Jesus."[78] In other words, Watson believed that the outpouring of the "latter rain" prompted sanctified Christians to "come out" and reestablish the New Testament church as a prelude to the second coming of Christ. Earlier during the great mid-century revival of 1857-1858, the English writer Catherine Marsh exhorted the church to "claim now the promise, 'the former rain' of which fell at Pentecost, when 3,000 souls were born to God in a day; and 'the latter rain' of which was to precede the second advent of our Lord and Saviour Jesus Christ."[79] The ramifications of the restorationist eschatology of the "latter rain" for the church created immeasurable excitement. But if the excitement and anticipation of the "latter rain" was immeasurable, its actual precipitation was fully quantifiable.

The classic work published on "latter rain" eschatology was D. Wesley Myland's *The Latter Rain Covenant* in 1910.[80] William D. Faupel notes that Myland followed the lead of radical holiness writers who came before him by "equating the early rain to justification and the latter rain to the Spirit-filled life."[81] This is especially evident in Martin Wells Knapp's book, *Out of Egypt into Canaan: Or Lessons in Spiritual Geography.* The realized eschatology of the radical Holiness movement stood in stark contrast to traditional Protestantism, which viewed the "Land of Promise as a type of heaven."[82] Knapp's personal conviction is made plain in the lyrics to the hymn "Sweet Rest of Canaan,"

> Once I thought this land of Canaan was a type of heaven above, But instead on earth I found it, In my Savior's perfect love.[83]

Myland argued for a similar understanding of the "latter rain," arguing that its outpouring would "bring back perfection and perpetuity to this fall-

---

77. Steven L. Ware, "Restoring the New Testament Church: Varieties of Restorationism in the Radical Holiness Movement of the Late Nineteenth and Early Twentieth Centuries," *Pneuma* 21, no. 2 (Fall 1999): 248.

78. Ibid., 248. See George D. Watson, *Types of the Holy Spirit* (Dallas: Evangel, n.d.), 70.

79. As quoted in Faupel, *The Everlasting Gospel,* 74.

80. David Wesley Myland, *The Latter Rain Covenant* (Chicago: Evangel Publishing House, 1910).

81. Faupel, *The Everlasting Gospel,* 34.

82. Ibid., 34.

83. Ibid., 34.

en world."[84] Reading Deut 11:21 as a prophetic verse, he believed it spoke of the time when the "latter rain" fell, "in the land which the Lord sware unto your fathers to give them, as the DAYS OF HEAVEN UPON THE EARTH (emphasis his)." He asked "when you get that rain of the Spirit upon you, don't you begin the days of heaven on the earth?"[85]

"Latter rain" theology was based on nine biblical passages.[86] Myland explained the importance of the "Latter Rain Covenant" for the church in their day:

> If it is remembered that the climate of Palestine consisted of two seasons, the wet and the dry, and that the wet season was made up of the early and latter rain, it will help you to understand the Covenant and the present workings of God's Spirit. For just as the literal early and latter rain was poured out upon Palestine, so upon the church of the First Century was poured out the spiritual early rain, and upon us today is being poured out the spiritual latter rain.[87]

Even though the exegetical focus of "latter rain" theology was placed on the spiritual nature of the rain, Myland considered it important to keep track of the literal rain falling in Palestine. The observation that earthly rain had increased significantly over the last half of the nineteenth century provided confirmation for the belief that the time of the spiritual "latter rain" was indeed upon them. Myland provided a chart at the end of his book that graphed the increase in rainfall in Palestine. He also explained the increase and its significance to his readers:

> Since 1860 the measurement of rain in Palestine has been recorded very accurately at Jerusalem, and shows a great increase, especially of the latter rain. It is a generally understood fact that for many centuries the rain-fall in Palestine was very small. During comparatively recent years the rain has been increasing. The official record of rain-fall, which was not kept until 1860, divides the time into ten-year periods, and the facts are that forty-three per cent more rain fell between the years 1890 and 1900 than fell from 1860 to 1870. . . . Spiritually the latter rain is coming to the church of God at the same time it is coming literally upon the land. . . .[88]

But what was important about the outpouring of the "latter rain" was its effect upon the church. The "first Pentecost *started* the church, the body of Christ, and this, the second Pentecost, *unites* and *perfects* the church unto the coming of the Lord (emphasis his)."[89] Thus, the "latter rain" eschatolo-

---

84. Myland, *Latter Rain Covenant*, 36.
85. Ibid., 37.
86. The nine passages include Deut 11:10-15; Job 29:29; Prov 16:15; Jer 3:3, 5:24; Hos 6:3; Joel 2:23; Zech 10:1; and Jas 5:7. By far the most important passage for "latter rain" advocates was Joel 2:23.
87. Myland, *Latter Rain Covenant*, 1.
88. Ibid., 94,95.
89. Ibid., 101.

gy provided for a new ecclesiological opportunity. In short, the "Church of God" had been restored to its original nature of holiness and unity in time for the return of Christ.

God was pouring out the "latter rain" and bringing about the "evening light," holiness folk believed, to prepare his bride for the soon return of his Son. An article in *The Revivalist* entitled "Relation of Holiness to the Return of Jesus," asked the question "Brother! have you the white robes on?" The author exhorted his readers to live a life of holiness in anticipation of the Second Coming. It may mean giving up respectability, friends and money, but seeing Jesus at his return was the reward. Otherwise, "you will be in a fine fix when He comes if you don't get holy."[90] Another *Revivalist's* writer warned sanctified believers to be ready for the coming of Christ. Even though they were robed they must be on the alert for "old Theater Go [who] may never come, but he sends his smooth-shaven stalwart son, Church Entertainment, to entice you away from your purpose."[91] Seth Rees reminded the holiness faithful that "without holiness no man shall see the Lord."[92] Martin Wells Knapp wrote these lyrics of caution in his song *The Midnight Cry*:

Have you taken the oil in your vessels?

Does the Spirit within you abide?

Are you cleansed in the blood ev'ry moment?

Are you watching and sanctified?

Soon, too late to prepare for the marriage,

Or ever admittance to gain;

Soon, the wise will with gladness have entered,

And the foolish stand knocking in vain.

(Chorus)

And oh, what a rapture and glory

will thrill thro' the heart of the Bride!

But oh, the despair and the anguish

Of those who stand knocking outside.[93]

---

90. H. C. Morrison, "Relation of Holiness to the Return of Jesus," *The Revivalist* (Cincinnati, Ohio) 11, no. 8 (August 1897): 2.

91. "Robed, Ready and Watching," *The Revivalist* (Cincinnati, Ohio) 11, no. 1 (January 5, 1899): 6.

92. Seth C. Rees, "Preparation for the Coming of the Lord," *The Revivalist* (Cincinnati, Ohio) 11, no. 2 (January 12, 1899): 6.

93. "The Midnight Cry," *The Revivalist* (Cincinnati, Ohio) 11, no. 6 (June 1897): 3.

The *Gospel Trumpet* proclaimed that "truly, nothing but entire purity can prepare us to joyfully meet the coming of Christ."[94] On the west coast, finally, the Southern California and Arizona Holiness Association also made it plain that "if we are His bride, without spot and blameless, we are ready for Him to come at any moment."[95]

The radical holiness church interpreted all doctrine through the rubric of holiness. And so it was with the Second Coming of Christ. Their stance on this matter was consistent with the requirement that entire sanctification be a prerequisite for fellowship. And even though it was not stated explicitly, the kind of holiness required to "see the Lord" must include the communal unity of the body of Christ. During the Azusa Street revival William J. Seymour fleshed out the aspects of interracial and multiethnic fellowship inherent in radical holiness doctrine and explicitly stated it as a preparation for the bride of Christ to meet her bridegroom.

Conclusion

The explicit restorationist nature within the radical holiness doctrines of sanctification and eschatology allowed the movement to reconsider its understanding of ecclesiology. No longer bound to church tradition, holiness folk turned to the scriptures to discover the church's divine template. In contradistinction to denominational Christianity, the saints contended that the composition of the New Testament church was holiness and unity, and its name the Church of God. This ecclesiological revelation provided sanctified Christians the opportunity to conceive a church organized counter to the prevailing religious and social customs of late nineteenth-century America. Embracing a conception of the body of Christ free from the exigencies of nineteen-hundred years of church history, the saints found themselves in a position to remake the church after the "biblical" model. As the next two chapters demonstrate, the development of sanctified unity ecclesiology and the practice of interracial and multiethnic fellowship exemplified how radical holiness folk employed the countercultural implications of their doctrines of sanctification and eschatology and transgressed the social mores of Jim and Jane Crowism.

---

94. "Are You Ready for His Coming?" *Gospel Trumpet* (Williamston, Michigan) 7, no. 16 (November 1, 1885): 3. Historian Merle Strege notes that "Warner, Schell, and those they influenced were certain of the world's imminent end on the basis of their interpretation of Old and New Testament apocalyptic." See Strege, *I Saw the Church*, 96.

95. L. A. Clark, "The Soon Coming King," *The Pentecost* 13th year no. 279 (November 12, 1897): 96.

Chapter Three

Sanctified Unity Ecclesiology: The Heart of the Radical Holiness Message

At the heart of radical holiness ecclesiology was the two-pronged message of unity and holiness. According to radical holiness orthodoxy, unity and holiness within the Church of God were a direct result of Wesleyan sanctification. No one could experience the transforming effects of the "double cure" and fail to seek fellowship with his or her Christian brother and sister. While holiness folk adhered to Martin Luther's theological insight that "salvation is by faith alone," their evaluation of the Protestant movement his teachings spawned was less than exuberant. Ranked only a notch above the detested Roman Catholicism, Protestantism had run aground on the shoals of schism. The denominationalism of Protestantism repudiated the very essence of Jesus' call for unity given in his high priestly prayer in John 17. And why had it not succeeded? Having recovered the biblical doctrine of *sola fide* from the dark medieval night, the reformation churches still lacked the critical New Testament tenet of holiness. George M. Teel, an elder and later president of the Southern California and Arizona Holiness Association, wrote in his book, *The New Testament Church*, that divisions were not allowed in the original church, but developed later "among the unsanctified."[1] It was sanctification, Jesus prayed in John 17, which made it possible for the church to be one. As a result, in the eyes of the saints Protestant sectarianism could not possibly be the Church of God about which the New Testament spoke.

The resultant theology of unity among believers that followed the experience of entire sanctification I have termed "sanctified unity" ecclesiology. The phrase sanctified unity is nowhere used in the books, journals and letters written by the saints. However, the ecclesiology of sanctified unity permeates the entire Holiness-Pentecostal movement during its early years.

---

1. Teel, *New Testament Church*, 32, 33.

The first part of sanctified unity ecclesiology, the desire to see the end of denominationalism and the reestablishment of a unified, and hence, holy Church of God, is well understood by scholars in the field of holiness studies. Indeed, it was at the forefront of radical holiness preaching and teaching. But what has not been fully appreciated by holiness and pentecostal scholars is how inclusive many Holiness-Pentecostals were in their understanding of the concept of unity. The writings of holiness radicals indicate that they believed multiethnic fellowship to be included under the rubric of one church. It is true that there is no systematic theology of interracial cooperation and equality that was produced by the Holiness-Pentecostal movement. William G. Schell's *Is the Negro a Beast? A Reply* is the book that comes nearest to espousing a theology of racial unity. But the purpose of his book was to counter Charles Carroll's racist polemic, *The Negro a Beast*, not to write on the ecclesiology of interracialism. Although no systematic theology exists, sprinkled throughout the corpus of Holiness-Pentecostal writings is a nascent theology arguing for the end of racial and ethnic divisions and the beginning of a new interracial fellowship within the Church of God.

Pursuing unity across the entire ethnic spectrum, then, is considered the second aspect, after the reconstituting of one ecclesiastical body, of sanctified unity ecclesiology. By combing over the primary Holiness-Pentecostal books and journals, this study reconstructs for the reader the ecclesiology of sanctified unity. Once sanctified unity ecclesiology is grasped, then the interracial and multiethnic fellowship practiced among the saints makes sense. Holiness folk made the Bible and theology a part of nearly all their discussions and the driving force of all their activities. So it should not be surprising to discover that a specific ecclesiological conception, what is termed here as sanctified unity ecclesiology, motivated black, white and brown saints to break the most important social taboo of their day and cross over the color line to fellowship with one other.

It is difficult to determine if the first adherents of radical holiness had any intention of forming a multiethnic church or if their message of unity simply acted as an irresistible elixir for the disenfranchised and marginalized minorities residing in late nineteenth-century America. Whichever the case, the holiness concept of unity quickly broadened beyond the scope of ecclesiastical wholeness and took on an interracial and multiethnic quality. The concept of one church soon crossed over the color line of segregationism then existing in the United States and became enamored with a countercultural church of "no Jew or Gentile, no woman or man, no slave or free" as written in Gal 3: 28.

The fact that whites, blacks and browns were able to defy the racist culture of their day demands a convincing explanation. One place to investigate for a potential answer is the lower social and economic class origins of the radical Holiness movement. As many have noted, the crossing of the color line among holiness radicals meant the interaction and fellowship of people from the lower economic class. It is the lower class, however, that historically has experienced the greatest amount of antagonism between the races.[2] So the answer is not likely to reside within the culture of the lower class.

Another avenue to explore for a possible explication is the rise of the Populist movement. Arising out of the same depressed elements of the lower class as the radical Holiness movement it might be convincingly demonstrated that Populism created the right political environment where self-interest intersected with interracial cooperation as the key motivating factor in bringing down the walls of segregation. C. Vann Woodward, in his classic *The Strange Career of Jim Crow*, proffered that during the initial ascension of the Populist movement cooperation between whites and blacks increased to a new plateau based on the common interest of self-interest. "This was an equalitarianism of want and poverty, the kinship of a common grievance and a common oppressor."[3] With the advent of the 1890s and the legislating of Jim Crow, Woodward argued that a sudden reversal took place in race relations.[4]

If Woodward's thesis is accepted it is tempting to postulate a connection between the cooperative race relations within Populism and the Holiness movement, since both movements appeared on the social scene at the same time. But two problems impede the acceptance of this proposition. First, since the publication of *The Strange Career of Jim Crow* scholarly opinion has formed a less favorable attitude towards Woodward's thesis of racial collaboration within the Populist movement leading up to a decisive break in the 1890s.[5] As Edward L. Wheeler has put it, "I tend . . . to agree with those historians who see the rise of legalized segregation as simply the institutionalization of long held racial views."[6] So whatever the political cooperation that did occur between blacks and whites it did little to eradicate the racial prejudice of lower class whites. Secondly, Norman K. Dann has demonstrated in his sociological and political study of the Populist and Holiness movements that there was no real causal connection between the two movements.[7] The one did not cause the other. His study establishes that although Populist politics and holiness religion occurred during the same time period, they did not significantly operate within the same geographic regions. Furthermore, Populist themes are not reflected in holiness journals. As a result, the "hypothesis that Populist activity concurrently

---

2. C. Vann Woodward, *The Strange Career of Jim Crow* (New York: Oxford University Press, 1974), 62.

3. Ibid., 61.

4. Ibid., 69.

5. Wheeler, *Uplifting the Race*, xix.

6. Ibid., xix.

7. Norman Kingsford Dann, "Concurrent Social Movements: A Study of the Interrelationships between Populist Politics and Holiness Religion" (Ph.D., diss., Syracuse University, 1974).

stimulated Holiness activity was rejected."[8] Thus, it is fair to conclude that the countercultural activity of the radical Holiness movement was not caused or significantly influenced by the political environment of the day, and certainly not by the American cultural milieu of the lower economic class.

This chapter will argue that understanding the ecclesiology of radical holiness devotees is determinative in grasping the motivation that led to the formation of multiethnic churches. Considering the saints' own words and conceptions of biblical truth as a legitimate explanation for their willingness to cross the social boundaries of Jim Crowism provides a plausible rationale for their actions. Holiness folk were deadly serious in their formulation of biblical theology. Once convinced of a biblical truth they applied all their efforts to making it a living reality in their own spiritual lives. So it is not surprising to discover that once they had become convinced that all persons, including minorities and women, were to be included in the very fabric of a unified church, they set their minds to making it an actuality. And this is what they did, not to the same degree in all the radical holiness churches, nor without periods of greater and lesser warmth towards each other and, sadly, not without it all coming apart in the end. But during the early days of the movement when the intensity of the movement was at its hottest, a countercultural paradigm based on Scripture seriously gripped the saints and urged them on to an egalitarianism that the church in America had never known.

The ecclesiology of sanctified unity became the hallmark of the radical Holiness movement. The two key passages of John 17 and Gal 3:28 came together to create a working definition of the true Church of God. Sanctification created the necessary and inevitable impulse towards unity among Christians be they black, brown, women or poor.

Sectism[9]

If one is to place a date on the first step towards an ecclesiology of sanctified unity, it must fall on March 7, 1878. On that otherwise inconspicuous day Daniel Warner entered these words into his diary:

> On the 31st of last January the Lord showed me that holiness could never prosper upon sectarian soil encumbered by human creeds and party names,

---

8. Ibid., 77, 78.

9. "Sectism" was a term used by the saints to refer to the problem of denominationalism in Protestantism. After his sermon on the ecclesiological unity of the Church of God was rejected by a group of African Americans in Charleston, South Carolina, J. F. Lundy observed that the "people here are under worse bondage in sectism and society than ever their ancestors under the taskmaster's lash in the dark days of slavery." J. F. Lundy and Co-workers, "News from the Field," *Gospel Trumpet* (Grand Junction) 16, no. 12 (March 19, 1896): 3.

and he gave me a new commission to join holiness and all truth together and build up the apostolic church of the living God. Praise his name! I will obey him.[10]

Just over three years later, in April 1881, God's revelation to Warner was reaffirmed when during a revival he mystically experienced the church in all its holiness and unity. In Warner's words he "saw the church." By June 1, 1881, Warner was telling the readers of the *Gospel Trumpet* that "we wish to cooperate with all Christians, as such, in saving souls-but forever withdraw from all organisms that uphold and endorse sects and denominations in the body of Christ."[11] Warner's actions thus birthed a nascent movement that persuaded countless thousands, black, white and brown, to leave their denominational churches and join the Church of God.

Warner, and those who adhered to a sanctified unity ecclesiology, taught that the sectarian nature of Protestantism was a great evil. H. M. Riggle, an early theologian in the Church of God Restoration Movement, gives a representative view in *The Christian Church: Its Rise and Progress*:

> For this cause there is perhaps no one thing more frequently enjoined in the New Testament than the oneness of all believers, no evil more peremptorily forbidden than that of schisms, and no sin more strongly denounced that that of causing division.[12]

Or as Charles Price Jones neatly summarized the problem, "Denominationalism is slavery."[13] They believed that the experience of sanctification, also referred to as the "baptism of the Holy Spirit," was the only cure for the divisive spirit that existed within sectarian churches. Certainly salvation was necessary for proper entry into the Church of God, but it did not destroy the fallen nature which was the cause of all divisions. Another early theologian in the Church of God Reformation Movement, F. G. Smith, described the problem, and cure, this way:

> While salvation itself brings us into a divine relationship with each other, the indwelling carnal nature prevents that perfect unity which Christ so much desired. . . . But sanctification purifies the heart, destroying carnality, and therefore makes the people of God "perfect in one. . . ."[14]

---

10. Smith, *Heralds of a Brighter Day*, 38.

11. Callen, *It's God's Church*, 92, 93.

12. H. M. Riggle, *The Christian Church: Its Rise and Progress* (Anderson, Ind.: Gospel Trumpet Company, 1912), 62.

13. Cobbins, *Church of Christ (Holiness)*, 27.

14. F. G. Smith, *What the Bible Teaches: A Systematic Presentation of the Fundamental Principles of Truth Contained in the Holy Scritures* (Guthrie, Okla.: Faith Publishing House, 1973), 226.

This basic belief in the ability of entire sanctification to produce a unified body of Christ is what set radical holiness adherents and their sanctified unity ecclesiology off from the larger Holiness movement. Advocates for the radical holiness message used John 17 as a proof-text for this position.[15] The larger Holiness movement made no attempt to dismantle Protestant denominations and call all Christians to one church. It was their hope that the message of personal holiness would work its way from the national and regional holiness camp meetings back into the mainstream churches and have a leavening effect upon them. The mainstream Holiness movement, in other words, never sought nor desired to apply the tenets of holiness theology to the corporate church. Personal "reform" was the watchword of the national Holiness movement which distanced them from the "come-outism" of radical holiness.[16]

In every corner of the radical Holiness movement, by way of contrast, the clear presentation of the ameliorating influence of entire sanctification was at the forefront of their preaching and writing. In an article printed in *The Burning Bush*, the official journal of the Metropolitan Church Association, the writer pronounced that "sanctified people are all one, one with Christ, and one with each other. They are all united by the blessing of sanctification, and nothing can separate them either from Christ or from each other except they backslide."[17]

Or again, Martin Wells Knapp, writing from Cincinnati in his ministry's paper, *The Revivalist*, matter-of-factly notes:

> Entire sanctification through the incoming of the Holy Ghost removes every jealousy and all obstructions to this union in the heart, and fills it with perfect love to God and man, so that henceforth union with all of God's people, of every name, is easy, natural and spontaneous.[18]

Across the nation all the saints agreed that entire sanctification provided the means through which Christians were able to fellowship as one, thereby fulfilling Jesus' prayer in John 17. J. F. Washburn, leader of the Southern California and Arizona Holiness Association, made explicit what was implicit in the radical Holiness movement doctrinal stance on church unity. Because the Church of God is built on holiness, the experience of the second grace of sanctification should be the standard for church fellowship. On February 5, 1886, Washburn wrote in the *Pentecost*, "The basis of membership in our church is entire sanctification and in order to retain their membership in the church each one must keep sanctified—this applies to the

---

15. The ubiquitous use of John 17 in radical holiness writings is truly astounding.

16. Dieter, *Holiness Revival*, 207-208.

17. "Holiness Machinery," *The Burning Bush*, (November 20, 1902): 6.

18. Martin Wells Knapp, "Pentecostal Union," *The Revivalist* 10 (November 1896): 2.

Elders as well as any one else. . . ."[19] No other radical holiness church followed the Southern California and Arizona Holiness Association in their decree, but *de facto*, if not *de jure*, the connection between the sanctified life, church fellowship, and church unity within all radical holiness churches was well established.[20]

Finally, similar sentiments regarding the curative effects of entire sanctification can be found in the southeastern section of the United States. G. F. Taylor, in his book *The Spirit and the Bride*, observed that holiness was preached "as the panacea for these ills" of disunity among the churches.[21] The Fire-Baptized Holiness Association of America, a Midwestern church led by Benjamin Irwin that made strong inroads into the Southeast, also taught that holiness was indispensable to Christian unity. In an article entitled "The Pentecostal Church," Irwin argued that the second mark of the Apostolic Church was unity, and using the New Testament church as his model noted that when "their hearts were cleansed and purified by the precious blood of Jesus . . . there was a oneness of spirit among them."[22]

The rest of this chapter will focus on the second facet of sanctified unity ecclesiology that shaped the beliefs and actions of the Holiness-Pentecostal church. It was their ecclesiology, I argue, more than anything else that provided the impetus for the crossing of the color line and equipped the saints to take the abuse, both mental and physical, that came their way for breaking the social taboos of their day. Their story is a great one even though it is little known. The courage to follow their biblical convictions has made them an example for how theological reflection can enable a people to rise above the present culture and provide an alternative socio-cultural model.

Crossing the Color Line

The capability of radical holiness adherents to think outside of the social mainstream of late nineteenth-century America begins and ends with theology. Just as sanctification was understood as the solution to the unholy divisions within Protestantism, similarly it provided the means for overcoming racial and ethnic animosity. Although proponents of entire sanctification were certainly open to charges of being naïve, it was this same naïveté that made the impossible seem possible to them. That is, the ability to imagine a new church where the barriers of race, gender and privilege did not exist. Even though sanctified unity ecclesiology developed during the

---

19. J. F. Washburn, "Sermon," *Pentecost* (Los Angeles) 1 (February 5, 1886): 2.

20. The Church of God Reformation Movement did not believe in church membership. Nevertheless, the experience or the desire to experience entire sanctification was necessary to "fellowship" with them.

21. G. F. Taylor, "The Spirit and the Bride," in *Three Early Pentecostal Tracts*, ed. Donald Dayton (New York: Garland, 1985), 49.

22. Benjamin Irwin, "The Pentecostal Church," *Live Coals of Fire* (Lincoln, Nebraska) 1 (June 1900): 2.

1880s when segregationism was still a nascent movement and some social flexibility still existed, it continued to be advocated—as this section demonstrates—during the next two decades when a nadir was reached in race relations.

Starting with Gal 3:28: "There is neither Jew nor Gentile, there is neither bond nor free, there is neither male nor female: for you are all one in Christ Jesus," along with its corollaries, Col 3:11, Rom 10:12, and 1 Cor 12:12, 13, 20, the heart of the second prong of sanctified unity ecclesiology is formed.[23] If in John 17 the church is told of the essential connection between sanctification and oneness, then Paul's provocative "neither Jew nor Gentile" passages signal the type of oneness that is intended within the Church of God. "The apostle [Paul] confessed that the Jews were no better than the Gentiles. Neither class had to come over to the other, but both to God through Christ Jesus. . . ."[24] The "neither Jew nor Gentile" passages frequently accompany discussions of and pleas for racial unity in radical holiness journals. Not unlike other exegetes in church history, they understood that the advent of the "new man" written about in Ephesians 2 meant an end to the historical, and even religious, divide between Jews and Gentiles. Moreover, the saints led the way in their willingness to relate directly the "neither Jew nor Gentile" passages to the social segregationism of late nineteenth-century America. But what made the radical Holiness movement unique was their readiness to put their ecclesiological convictions into practice—to have people of all races worship together as one. No longer simply perceived as a rarified theological discussion about the division between the "chosen people" and the Gentile nations, radical holiness believers applied the Pauline passages to the present disunity among black and white believers.[25] When they read the "neither Jew nor Gentile" passages they believed it applied to the immediate race problem in the United States. Literally, "Jew and Gentile" translated into "white and black." For example, when J. E. Shaw, his wife and W. E. Gillespie reported back to the *Gospel Trumpet* on their work in Georgia, they stated: "We love our race and want to see them saved, but if they reject the Gospel we will have to do like the Apostles, turn to the (colored) Gentiles. The devil has a big thing in this

---

23. Church of God (Anderson) historian Merle D. Strege concludes in his book, *I Saw the Church*, that the "pattern of racial unity in the [Church of God Reformation] movement's early decades was driven by a literal reading of Galatians 3:28 as the normative status of the true New Testament church." Strege, *I Saw the Church*, 147.

24. Riggle, *The Christian Church*, 52.

25. The social division between blacks and whites was deeper and longer in American history and so received the most attention. But as the membership rolls and journal articles suggest, the Pauline passages also applied to a larger ethnic division in American society that included Native Americans, Latinos and Asians, not to mention Jews.

race, prejudice in the South, and in some places in the North, too, we guess."[26] In the second of two articles entitled "National Prejudice" written for the *Gospel Trumpet* in 1898, George Cole noted that when the gospel was first preached the assembly of believers was not divided along national lines. Citing Gal 3:28, he argued that the separation of the races in his own day was, therefore, contrary to the original gospel message. Not content to critique simply the segregationism then prevailing in the church, Cole called for a direct response. Those who preach a gospel that divides the church according to race "are to be avoided."[27] Cole's rationale is straightforward, "neither will we please God nor reform any one if we follow the customs of prejudiced hearts through compromise, which is . . . hypocrisy."[28] Even as late as 1917, when much of the Church of God Reformation Movement had already compromised with Jim Crowism, an article appeared in the *Gospel Trumpet* making the argument for "brotherly love and spiritual harmony" among the races based on the "neither Jew nor Gentile" passages of Galatians and Colossians.[29] Although the article's message was written ultimately in vain, it demonstrates the prevalent exegetical connection within radical holiness circles between the American conception of race and the Pauline two-race designation.

George Goings, an African-American holiness evangelist to the South for the Southern California and Arizona Holiness Association, also made the common link between "whites and blacks" and "Jews and Gentiles."[30] Writing in *The Pentecost* in 1897, Goings described the horrible conditions, spiritual and material, which he found among southern blacks. Noting the lack of public interaction that occurred between blacks and whites, he explained that "owing to former and present training they are as separate from the white race among whom they dwell as the Jew is from the Gentiles."[31] Using Gal 3:27-28 as his biblical text, Martin Wells Knapp argued in *Lightening Bolts from Pentecostal Skies* that the baptism of the Holy Spirit was for all nationalities. "Sammy Morris, the Kru boy; David of India, and Amanda

---

26. J. E. Shaw, "News from the Field," *Gospel Trumpet* (Grand Junction) 14 (May 1894): 3.

27. George L. Cole, "National Prejudice," *Gospel Trumpet* (Moundsville, W.Va.) 18 (December 8, 1898): 2.

28. Ibid., 2.

29. *Gospel Trumpet*, "Observations of Our Times," (August 30, 1917): 544.

30. I thank David Daniels for the astute observation that among African-American holiness radicals blacks were often equated with Jews and whites with Gentiles, just the opposite of white holiness radicals. Perhaps it is fair to say that while both white and black saints advocated an equalitarian fellowship between the two races, each still wanted to be first among equals.

31. George A. Goings, "How Shall We Reach Them?" *Pentecost* (Los Angeles), 13th Year, no. 263 (March 26, 1897): 30.

Smith, the sanctified slave, are among the many modern proofs of this truth."[32] He makes the same point later on in the book when after citing Gal 3:28 again he asserts that "barriers of race, and color, and social position have no true place in Christ's Church."[33]

When in 1900 Charles Carroll wrote his infamous polemic against black people, *The Negro a Beast*,[34] editors of the *Gospel Trumpet* indicated that some "of the dear brethren have read this book and have been bothered somewhat about it, and have written us about it."[35] The disturbed saints sought a rebuttal from the Church of God Reformation Movement's leadership. *Gospel Trumpet* editor William Schell provided it with a book-length response. His *Is the Negro a Beast? A Reply*, attempted to dismantle Carroll's argument on scientific, historical and theological grounds. After postulating that John 17 demonstrated God's desire for unity within the church and that the experience of sanctification made it possible, he centered his theological reply on Carroll's prejudice against blacks using Gal 3:28, Rom 10:12, 13, and Col 3:11, all Pauline "neither Jew nor Gentile" passages. Like J. E. Shaw, he did not merely attempt to prove Carroll, and his kind, wrong, but declared that "such downright prejudice and hatred against the colored races would bar any human soul out of heaven and [send] it to eternal damnation...."[36]

J. O. McClurkan, leader of the Pentecostal Mission in Nashville, Tennessee, in 1901 makes the same link between the Pauline call for Jews and Gentiles to be one and the American race problem. In *Zion's Outlook*, the mission's paper, he made this clear proclamation:

> Thank God that holiness is the great resolvent of this problem. The sanctified heart is absolutely cleansed of all war or race prejudice. Holiness deepens and sweetens and broadens the nature until every man of all and every section and nationality and color and condition is loved as a brother. There is no North, no South, no Jew, no Greek, no Barbarian to be sanctified. We be brethren. "For by one spirit are we all baptized into one body, whether it be Jews or Gentiles, whether we be bond or free, and have been all made to drink into one spirit." 1 Cor. 12: 13.[37]

Finally, a co-worker with McClurkan and co-founder of the Church of God in Christ, Charles Price Jones, an African-American, described the unity

---

32. Knapp, *Lightening Bolts*, 25.

33. Ibid., 173.

34. Charles Carroll, *The Negro a Beast* (Miami, Fla.: Mnemosyne Publishing Co., 1900).

35. William G. Schell, "The Negro a Beast," *Gospel Trumpet*, 21, no. 21 (May 23, 1901): 4.

36. William G. Schell, *Is the Negro a Beast? A Reply to Charles Carroll's Book Entitled 'The Negro a Beast,' Proving That the Negro Is Human from Biblical, Scientific, and Historical Standpoint* (Moundsville, W.Va.: Gospel Trumpet Publishing Company, 1901), 139, 154.

37. J. O. McClurkan, "That They May Be One," *Zion's Outlook* (February 7, 1901): 8.

at a holiness convention held in the South in 1897 this way, "for those who labored with singleness of heart Christ was all and in all. Black and white, Jew and Gentile sought God together."[38]

There is one other Pauline passage dealing with the relationship between Jews and Gentiles that should be considered before moving on to other scriptural passages interpreted to support the notion of racial and ethnic unity. The second chapter of Ephesians was used quite often when making the argument that Christ had torn down the barrier between Jews and Gentiles. The heart of chapter two are verses fourteen through sixteen, "for he [Christ] is our peace, who hath made both [Jew and Gentile] one, and hath broken down the middle wall of partition . . . that he might reconcile both unto God in one body, by the cross, having slain the enmity thereby." Perhaps the most famous application of this passage was made during an 1897 revival in Hartselle, Alabama, when Lena Cooper, female evangelist for the Church of God Reformation Movement, preached a message on tearing down the wall of partition between the Jews and Gentiles. The message was addressed to a mixed audience of blacks and whites. As was the Jim Crow custom of the day whites and blacks sat in their respective sections, divided from each other by a rope. It seems that at some point in her sermon Cooper sought to demonstrate the meaning of the wall of partition coming down between Jews and Gentiles. Applying the Ephesians passage to her own context, Cooper, like so many others in the radical Holiness movement, equated biblical Jew and Gentile with white and black. This led her to unhook the rope and call blacks and whites to the altar where they freely intermingled with each other in prayer. The reaction of the local population was such that later that night the revival platform was blown up with dynamite and the evangelists were forced to flee for their lives. Most found safety in the homes of those friendly to the revival, but one evangelist was forced into donning women's clothing to escape the persecution meant for him, and another stood in a creek all night.[39]

George L. Cole, in his seminal articles on the race problem in 1898, understood that the time had come to end racial and national prejudice in saintly circles since the "middle wall of partition is broken down between us." He knew that intermixing with other "classes" caused a great amount of discomfort, and that the social pressure not to break social taboos created a lot of apprehension. But the answer did not reside in disunity among the nations, but in applying more of "the precious blood of Jesus," a common reference to entire sanctification in radical holiness circles.[40]

---

38. Cobbins, *History of Church of Christ (Holiness)*, 28. Later, at the Azusa Street revival, *The Apostolic Faith* paper will make the same connection between the "neither Jew nor Gentile" passages and the racial unity experienced during the revival.

39. Smith, *Holiness and Unity*, 164-165.

40. Cole, "National Prejudice," 2.

The African-American holiness evangelist George Goings moved to the South to preach holiness to underserved blacks in that area. He reported back to *The Pentecost* that at their meetings "some white Holiness preachers are rendering valuable service." That whites were reaching out to the black population in the South was of great encouragement to him. For some time he had been rebuking the holiness church for caring more for the people of Africa than for the millions of their descendents now living in what he pejoratively called the "land of Bibles."[41] As a result, he alluded to Ephesians 2 and John 17 when he noted that "God has through His fire-baptized servants, male and female, whom He sent, broken down the partition wall. . . . I do praise God for the sweet peace and harmony that has existed and that is what astonishes the world."[42]

The Pauline passages calling for a new accord between Jews and Gentiles provided the basis for the radical holiness argument that race and ethnicity should not be a dividing wall within the church.[43] The biblical literalism that guided the radical holiness hermeneutic on a personal level also applied communally to the church. Just as the Jews had to accept the Gentiles into the church on an equal status, so whites were commanded to do the same with their black and brown brothers and sisters. The hermeneutical approach of the saints allowed them to make a literal application of the first-century writings of the Bible to their own day. James W. McClendon refers to this interpretative approach to reading the Bible as "this is that."[44] This is a helpful phrase on two accounts: first, it directly quotes Peter in Acts 2 when he equated the events at Pentecost with the Joel 2 prophecy, and second, this phrase was used quite regularly by Holiness-Pentecostals when explaining the connection between events in their own time and the first-century church. In short, "this is that" was held as a presuppositional

---

41. Washburn, *History and Reminiscences*, 92, 368.

42. Ibid., 340.

43. One intriguing example involves a controversy over the admission of African Americans to Pauline Holiness College(PHC). Founded by the radical Holiness Church of God (Holiness)in Missouri, PHC encountered opposition over its admission policy in 1886. Letters to the college informed the school's administration that some southern people found the interracial arrangement offensive to their social ordering. B. A. Washburn's reply begins by chastising any sanctified believer who still harbors prejudicial feelings towards blacks. Then in what seems to be an inference to the "no Jew or Gentile" foundation of sanctified unity ecclesiology he writes, "If Pauline College is true to *name* then it would be looked upon as a blessing and of God. But, if you exclude a part of the human family from its benefits, how can you hope to have His favor(emphasis mine)?" A short time later the school board convened and issued a policy statement: "Resolved, that it is the sense of this Association that Pauline Holiness College is open to all people who will come to avail themselves of its educational advantages, and who will comply strictly with the terms of its constitution, and that no race distinction will be made in its future administration." See Cowen, *Church of God (Holiness)*, 35.

44. McClendon, *Systematic Theology*, 31.

belief among holiness folk to substantiate that their church was the literal New Testament church.

In reading the writings of the saints one also detects among whites a strong identification with the Jews of the Bible. Perhaps this stems from the commonly held belief that America was a kind of new Promised Land for the first English settlers. Consequently, whites considered themselves as direct participants in America's divine destiny and nonwhites as outsiders. So the conceptual framework out of which most whites operated made it an easy transition to see themselves (Jews) as the ones to welcome blacks (Gentiles) into the fold. Both on hermeneutical and historical levels, then, the "neither Jew nor Gentile" passages connected to the self-perception of the white saints and provided the key description for the racial makeup of the recently reestablished Church of God.

The point is that the call to break down the wall of partition expressed in Ephesians 2 persuaded holiness folk that unity should prevail between all nationalities and races. This is evidenced in the fact that the radical holiness movement directed a not inconsiderable amount of their energy to this critical insight.[45]

The writings of Paul were not the only sections of Scripture from which the ecclesiology of sanctified unity was derived. The story of Peter's interaction with the Gentile Cornelius was a favorite passage used to demonstrate that God did not favor one people over another. In Acts 10:34 Peter states, "I perceived that God is no respecter of persons; but in every nation he that feareth him, and worketh righteousness, is accepted with him."[46] To

---

45. See Riggle, *The Christian Church*, 52, 53; Smith, *What the Bible Teaches*, 225; *Gospel Trumpet* 37, no. 51 "Questions Answered" (December 27, 1917): 3; *Pentecost* (Los Angeles) 391 "Holiness and Unity," (May 22, 1896), 42; Teel, *New Testament Church*, 63; and Reed, "Toward the Integrity," 166. Reed highlights the desire of Commissioner Railton of the Salvation Army who, as Reed has put it, believed that the Army would "faithfully and wholly break down the wall of partition" between the races.

46. Donald Mathews, Milton C. Sernett and James Melvin Washington all agree that Acts 10 was an oft used passage among slaves to prove their essential equality with whites. Unfortunately, the sources do not exist to demonstrate adequately the contribution that slave religion made to sanctified unity ecclesiology. The theological reflection among blacks pertaining to interracialism that did develop in the second half of the nineteenth century evolved almost solely out of their independent Baptist and Methodist traditions. In general, they argued for the equality of the races on the broad theological principle of the "Fatherhood of God and the brotherhood of man." They took this argument over from the social gospel movement without accepting the biblical criticism of that movement. See Donald Mathews, *Religion in the Old South* (Chicago: The University of Chicago Press, 1977), 219; Milton C. Sernett, *Black Religion and American Evangelicalism* (Metuchen, N.J.: Scarecrow Press, 1975), 108; James Melvin Washington, *Frustrated Fellowship: The Black Baptist Quest for Social Power* (Macon, Ga.: Mercer University Press, 1986), 27; Paris, *Social Teaching*, 10.

the saints, Acts 10 was simply another example of God breaking down the wall of division between a Jew and a Gentile. One history of the Church of God in Christ, a predominantly black Holiness-Pentecostal group, explained the cause of the interracial makeup of its early leadership as a byproduct of the Azusa Street revival, since the "Holy Ghost fell on Azusa Street on a mixed congregation, thus proving the thing God tried to show to Peter that he is no respecter of person, no racial God, but a God of every nation Bless His Name."[47] Alluding to Acts 10, A. H. Dugdale wrote to the *Pentecost* "God has respect only to personal character in the acceptance of men. Poverty, illiteracy, physical disability do not debar men from God's bounties; neither are national . . . distinctions of any account with God."[48] Meeting in 1883, the Southern California and Arizona Holiness Association ruled that the "God of Heaven has raised up the holy people (Isa. 60:12) out of various sects and nationalities and without regard to either, He being no respecter of persons. . . ."[49] Martin Wells Knapp also stated that the baptism of the Holy Spirit is no respecter of persons. It falls "in defiance of color, clime, creed, and social, political or ecclesiastical position. . . ."[50] Finally, in *Is the Negro a Beast? A Reply*, William G. Schell also used the encounter between Peter and Cornelius to illustrate that all nations were to hear the gospel and be received into the Church of God.[51]

Radical Holiness evangelists and theologians continued to link the "neither Jew nor Gentile" theme to other scriptural passages. Theologian H. M. Riggle, for example, employed the words of Jesus in John 10:16 to argue for unity among different nationalities. "Other sheep I have, which are not of this fold: them also I must bring, and they shall hear my voice; and there shall be one fold, and one shepherd." Riggle maintained that John 10:16 was a clear call on the part of Jesus to bring Jews (this fold) and Gentiles (other sheep) into unity (one fold). Reflecting on the majority sentiment in his own day that differences between blacks and whites should perpetuate the separation of the races, Riggle noted that the same problem existed in the time of Jesus,

> between these two classes [Jews and Gentiles] was a great gulf of prejudice and vast separation in sentiment and education, so that it might very reasonably be thought that characters so remote from each other could never

47. Lucille Cornelius, comp., *The Pioneer: History of the Church of God in Christ* (n.p., 1975), 16.

48. A. H. Dugdale, "Peter and Cornelius," *Pentecost* (Los Angeles) 391 (April 18, 1902): 4.

49. Washburn, *History and Reminiscences*, 53, 54.

50. Knapp, *Lightening Bolts*, 9.

51. Schell, *Negro a Beast*, 137.

be blended together in one body and enabled to live agreeably under one faith.[52]

According to John 10:16, Riggle postulated, the solution was not to be found in separate churches but in the solidarity brought through salvation in Jesus Christ. The statement of Christ "and there shall be one fold" was a commandment. Accordingly, Riggle concluded,

> did, therefore, the Lord indulge their alienation from each other, and their extreme peculiarities, by providing separate folds? He did not. . . .Then, for all the saved of the nations of the earth God has provided but 'one fold.' In it are peacefully blended together men of the most widely conflicting idiosyncrasies, and races of the most opposite customs. . . .[53]

In Southern California, finally, the holiness leader B. A. Washburn also utilized John 10:16 to argue for unity among all Christians. Published in *The Pentecost* on Christmas day in 1886, Washburn's article "The Unity of the Spirit" brought together Jesus' call for "one fold" and the "neither Jew nor Gentile" passage in 1 Cor 12:13 to declare that Spirit baptism "brings people into harmony." It is a lack of scriptural understanding and human understanding, Washburn proffered, that breaks the beautiful chain linking "nationalities" and "color."[54]

To summarize, the development of sanctified unity ecclesiology began with a critique of the many denominational divisions within Protestantism. Indeed, based on John 17 the preponderance of discussion involving sanctified unity revolved around the issue of ecclesiastical disunity. First and foremost, radical holiness adherents desired to see the corporate union of the saints in the one, true Church of God. In the eyes of holiness folk, denominationalism was sectism, the most egregious of sins since it ran directly counter to Jesus' high priestly prayer for unity as a witness to the world. As a result, the "threshing of Babylon" and the establishment of the church on the New Testament model became the first order of business.

The record demonstrates that early on in the radical Holiness movement, African Americans and other ethnic groups found the sanctified unity message of oneness among believers particularly appealing. The message was based on a theological understanding that Jews and Gentiles were to fellowship as one. The opportunity to overcome the long history of being second-class citizens within the Kingdom of God prompted many to abandon their former churches and take up residence in the emerging radical holiness associations. The evidence also supports the fact that whites equally welcomed minorities into their ranks, and this during a time when Jim Crowism was steadily gripping the nation.

---

52. Riggle, *The Christian Church*, 52.

53. Ibid., 52, 53.

54. B. A. Washburn, "The Unity of the Spirit," *Pentecost* (Los Angeles) 16 (December 25, 1886): 4.

Chapter Four

Living Holiness on the Other Side
of the Color Line

The development of sanctified unity ecclesiology undergirded and induced the practice of interracial and multiethnic fellowship within radical Holiness churches. Primary source research demonstrates that different degrees of interaction took place between black, brown and white saints in the major radical holiness locations of Southern California, Midwest, upper South and Southeastern sections of the United States. In each location sanctified unity ecclesiology supported, justified, even commanded that the oneness of the church meant more than the mere corporate unity of the church, but must be defined by the acceptance, indeed, the fellowshipping together of all races, nations and ethnicities. The record suggests that this is what the saints did. To be sure, there were limitations placed on interracial and multiethnic fellowship. The most notable restriction prohibited mixed-race marriages.[1] Even the most ardent propagators of sanctified unity ecclesiology were opposed to interracial marriage. Critics of interracial fellowship typically charged that holiness folk not only wanted to have church with blacks but believed in the amalgamation of the races. The saints responded that the biblical prescription for church unity did not automatically mean that the races should come together in matrimony. George L. Cole, a strong advocate of sanctified unity ecclesiology, called the charge of amalgamation made against holiness teaching a "falsehood." Rather, the acceptance of the holiness message will remove the desire for fornication and adultery from the heart which is the real cause of amalgama-

---

1. The best-known holiness community to support mixed marriages officially was John Alexander Dowie's Zion community in Illinois. But even here the views of an authoritarian leader failed to overcome the deep-seated conviction against miscegenation. When a black man and white woman availed themselves of Dowie's progressive teaching they were "run out of town" by members of the Zion community. Story related to author during a guided tour of the Dowie house in the fall of 2003.

tion. But that was not all, "when saved people want to marry it will be natural for each to desire a companion of their own nationality, and it will be thus when all prejudice is taken out of the hearts."[2] A *Gospel Trumpet* editorial in 1912 also drew the line at interracial marriage. "Doubtless it has been God's design that there should be the various races and colors of people; therefore, we ought to recognize this fact and to avoid amalgamation."[3] The objection to interracial marriage was widely accepted throughout the radical Holiness movement. On this account, they were in complete agreement with the social mores of the larger American culture. Nevertheless, the degree to which they practiced interracial and multiethnic fellowship put them at odds with American racial attitudes, so much so that the charge of amalgamation persisted in the perception of outsiders in spite of the saints' objections.

From the very outset of the radical Holiness movement whites welcomed blacks, Native Americans and other ethnic groups into their revivals. Persecution often interrupted the revivals as a result of the racial mixing that went on during the meetings. In 1890 Daniel Warner was preaching in Mississippi to a racially diverse crowd when a mob of seventy-five whites appeared to disrupt the service. During the meeting a brick smashed through a window and hit Warner in the head. With blood dripping from his head Warner and those present fled the scene and escaped to nearby cabins and homes for safety. After this event Warner was inspired to write the hymn "Who will suffer with the Savior?"[4]

In an editorial in his holiness journal, *Live Coals of Fire*, Benjamin Irwin reflected on the racial animosity he faced from both whites and blacks while preaching in Abbeville, South Carolina. "In this country the proud, supercilious, ungodly Whites look upon us with scorn and contempt because we hold meetings for the colored people, and preach the gospel to their former slaves; and some of them look at us as though they would like to burn us at the stake for carrying the "unsearchable riches of Christ" to the hungry blacks. . . .On the other hand, the unholy hypocritical negroes persecuted the sanctified ones amongst them of "drinking out of white-mouthed bottles." Carnality is the same in all ages, in all nations, and peoples."[5]

Finally, Holiness-Pentecostal preacher Richard Baxter Hayes made it a practice to involve blacks and whites in his services. When the time came for the altar call he refused to follow the social mores of the South and allowed whites and blacks to seek God together at an integrated altar. In 1898, in Madison County, Georgia, during a service a "large man accosted

2. George L. Cole, "National Prejudice," *Gospel Trumpet* (Moundsville, W.Va.) 18 (December 1, 1898): 1.

3. "Evidence of Race Prejudice," *Gospel Trumpet* 32 (March 21, 1912): 178.

4. Callen, *It's God's Church*, 124.

5. Benjamin Irwin, "Editorial," *Live Coals of Fire* (Lincoln, Nebraska) 1, no. 5 (November 3, 1899): 1.

the preacher with a stick for 'showing Negro equality.'" Using the moment to demonstrate the power of God, Hayes informed the man that God "would strike him dead if he hit him. The man turned pale, dropped his stick and went away." Hayes' display of spiritual and physical courage ignited a revival that swept through the local black communities, causing the establishment of several new fellowships for the Pentecostal Holiness Church and the Fire-Baptized Holiness Church.[6]

For African Americans and other ethnic groups accustomed to the harsh realities of Jim Crow laws, interracial participation at radical holiness revivals came as a welcome surprise. It takes little imagination to hear the wonderment that Laura Goings, wife of George Goings, experienced during a camp meeting in Monrovia, California:

> This is a queer camp. I sometimes look on with amazement. Five distinct races or nationalities, three generations (and some between), diversities of make-up, religious training, temperament, etc., yet God enables us to keep in *perfect harmony, without an effort to do so.* Only God could do it. Hallelujah! (emphasis hers)[7]

The central radical holiness theme of forging oneness out of diversity is quite evident in Mrs. Goings' letter. The extraordinary unity experienced among holiness Christians from diverse church and racial backgrounds only reinforced the wonder-working power of the sanctified life. W. A. Caleb, a Native American and evangelist for the Southern California and Arizona Holiness Association, wrote from Plattsburg, Missouri that after whites, Indians and blacks were brought to faith, "Plattsburg was dismayed when told God was no respecter of persons."[8]

The color line was traversed frequently during radical holiness revival meetings. Church of God (Anderson) historian Merle D. Strege observes:

> It was not uncommon for members of both ethnic groups to attend the same tent meetings and revivals, on occasion drawing the ire of local residents for transgressing such racial taboos as mixed seating. In some instances Whites served as ministers in biracial gatherings; in other cases Black ministers took the lead.[9]

Thus, blacks were not only part of a mixed audience at radical holiness revivals but also provided some of the most dynamic preachers.

One of the great preachers within the Metropolitan Church Association (MCA) was "Black Susan" Fogg. As part of the "white horse riders," she barnstormed all over New England preaching the gospel of holiness. By

---

6. Vinson Synan, *The Old-Time Power*, 149.
7. Mrs. G. A. Goings, *Pentecost* (Los Angeles), 12th Year, no. 243 (July 1896): 59.
8. W. A. Caleb, "Account of Open Air Work," *Pentecost* (Los Angeles) 299 (August 5, 1898): 65.
9. Strege, *I Saw the Church*, 146-147.

1903 she was the MCA's most celebrated preacher. According to MCA scholar William Kostlevy, there were many African-American preachers in the MCA and the MCA conventions were "racially integrated." E. L. Harvey, a key leader in the movement, was known for his special concern for minorities and the socially marginalized.[10] As for Sister Fogg she left the MCA at the height of her popularity for an MCA mission in India.[11]

Charles Mason, African-American leader of the Church of God in Christ, regularly preached to mixed audiences. Noted for his high character and amiable personality, Mason was genuinely liked and respected by almost everyone. As a result the white leadership of cities such as Nashville and Little Rock invited him to lead revivals in their cities. Mason summed up his life as a gospel minister stating that the "Spirit through me has saved, sanctified and baptized thousands of souls of all colors and nationalities."[12]

Leadership roles during revivals and camp meetings did not end at the pulpit, but blacks also gave needed guidance and prayer to those in spiritual need. Howard Goss, a worker in Charles Parham's Apostolic Faith movement, penned these words in his personal diary on August 14, 1906, "Glorious meeting, and a colored woman prayed for me and I received the tongues."[13] In Cincinnati, black participants at Martin Wells Knapp's Holiness Union meetings were emboldened to invite white folks to their groups' revival meetings. Once during a meeting led by Seth C. Rees a traveling man came to the revival on the invitation of a black porter he had met earlier that day. Convicted by the Spirit, the stranger made his way to the altar that night and received victory over sin.[14]

The workers in Cincinnati made no secret of their desire to break down the walls of class and race. Once when Knapp was put on trial for disturbing the peace during his revival meetings, Mary Storey, a mission worker, was asked the question, "Whom do you labor for the benefit of?" She replied, "Everybody, rich and poor, high and low, black and white."[15] The tes-

---

10. A group picture in the March 3, 1904 edition of *The Burning Bush* issue reveals black men and women interspersed in a largely white assembly. *The Burning Bush* (March 3, 1904).

11. Kostlevy, "Nor Silver, Nor Gold," 185, 186, 274. One remarkable story of Harvey's deep concern for the dispossessed relates how he hired a lawyer to help a falsely accused black man gain acquittal on the charge of murder. Years later at Harvey's funeral the African-American man broke down sobbing, prostrating himself next to the coffin repeating the words "no one ever loved me like that man."

12. Mary Mason, *The History and Life Work of Elder C. H. Mason and His Co-Laborers* (n.p., 1924), 31-32.

13. Howard Goss, "Travel Diary," (n.p.) (August 14, 1906), n.p. Located at the Assemblies of God's Flower Pentecostal Heritage Center.

14. *The Revivalist* (Cincinnati, OH) "Cincinnati, Ohio" 11, no. 1 (January 5, 1899): 12.

15. Hills, *A Hero of Faith and Prayer*, 248.

timonies of African-American saints printed in *The Revivalist* best tell the story.

"Jesus picked me up three months ago and placed my feet on the solid rock. He has taken me out of the bar room, out of the saloon, and now I serve God instead of the devil. I was a member of the Baptist Church, thought I was a Christian man, but I was a partaker of these things; my deacon went with me to the saloon, too. When I came here and heard this people talking of being saved from those things, I saw that I was not living a Christian life, so I repented and left all those things behind. . . ."[16]

Another African-American brother expressed the powerful effects of Knapp's ministry on him by noting:

> I have such a long testimony this afternoon, I guess I will have to save it, and breathe it out on the street corner this evening. Saved and sanctified, I am proud of it too. The devil has no chance at my heart.[17]

One compelling example of what might transpire between different races during revival meetings involved Laura Goings. Speaking at the Salvation Army one night a white lady in the audience experienced a new profound love for African Americans. Reared in Missouri during the time of slavery she was prejudiced against blacks and their religious ways. But that night the Spirit enabled her to die to her prejudice. Seeking to demonstrate her new-found freedom she invited Mrs. Goings to the Free Methodist Church, her home church. Laura Goings was permitted to give an exhortation to the church at which point the white "sister testified, shouted and confessed that she loved me, which she demonstrated to the surprise of all who knew her." For Mrs. Goings it was further proof that "the clean word will cut off all superfluities."[18]

As B. Scott Lewis notes, followers of Daniel Warner wrote into the *Gospel Trumpet* to report that one key outcome of a person's salvation and sanctification was the end of prejudice in the heart.[19] W. J. Henry represented this view well in a December 20, 1906 article in the *Gospel Trumpet*:

> There is no room for prejudice of any kind in the hearts of sanctified people. If you, as a white man find any of this in your heart toward a black man as an individual or toward his people, you need to go to the Lord for cleansing; to the black brother, I will say the same. All prejudice of every kind is outside the church of God.[20]

---

16. "Coals from Cincinnati Meeting," *The Revivalist* (Cincinnati, Ohio) 11, no. 23 (June 8, 1899): 4.

17. "Testimonies," *The Revivalist* 12, no. 17 (April 26, 1900): 4.

18. Washburn, *History and Reminiscences*, 305.

19. *Gospel Trumpet* (August 25, 1898), 5 and (April 26, 1900), 5.

Lewis summarizes this evangelistic approach well as souls "saved, sanctified, and prejudice removed."[21]

Holiness folk likewise did not tolerate any breach in the practice of sanctified unity. Once a person had claimed entire sanctification it was expected that the fruit of sanctified unity ecclesiology would be demonstrated in his or her life. When this did not happen then corrective action was taken. J. G. Lundy wrote the *Gospel Trumpet* from Anderson, South Carolina, about the problems among the saints involving racial mixing at meetings. When word spread to whites in the surrounding area that an interracial meeting was taking place, they accused the adherents of holiness of trying to establish "Negro equality!" When some of the whites buckled under to the local pressure, Lundy did not hesitate in his response. Lundy's account relates the direction the holiness leadership took with the wayward members:

> God most wonderfully used this thing to purge the assembly of the people. Quite a number were professing entire sanctification at this place, testifying that nothing could ever move them, not even the burning stake. But when this little test of their reputation in the estimation of the people came up, although it was far short of the flames, it showed up several who were not where they testified to be. The devil had run in a compromise policy and God was not pleased. He knew that there were too many here for God to get glory, many professing to be saints, who were not right at heart; hence the purging.[22]

Lundy considered the result to be a positive one. The essential unity of the meeting was paramount if the group was to profess holiness boldly. He concluded by drawing a direct link between sanctification and sanctified unity ecclesiology.

"This meeting was one of glorious victory. Some dead branches were purged out and now the church moves without these hindrances. This test on the color line showed the difference between sanctified souls and professors of such. Some were filled with malice and prejudice and yet professing to be sanctified, whereas they were not even justified. . . . May God wake the people up to the Bible standard."[23]

George Cole likewise argued that sanctification and racial prejudice could not co-exist in a genuine saint.

"How can we have confidence in people's profession of sanctification when there are marks, manifestations, and feelings of prejudice, whether it be against the Africans, Chinese, Spanish, Egyptians, Jews, or the poor of our

---

20. W. J. Henry, "The Color Line" in *Gospel Trumpet* (December 20, 1906), 3.

21. B. Scott Lewis, "William J. Seymour: Follower of the 'Evening Light' (Zech. 14:7)," *Wesleyan Theological Journal* 39, no. 2 (Fall 2004), 172.

22. J. F. Lundy, "News from the Field," *Gospel Trumpet* (Grand Junction, Mich.) 15, no. 33 (August, 22, 1895): 3.

23. Ibid., 3.

own race? Salvation must and will bring God's people into fellowship and communion in the Holy Spirit, regardless of nationality."[24]

In a two-part article entitled "Unity of Believers," Martin Wells Knapp reminded his readership that "when you were converted God put this love [for others] into your heart; then when you were sanctified wholly He perfected it in you."[25] But what happens when the saints begin to lose their first love? Knapp reflects on the matter, "when you began to lose your first love you didn't want to go to the same meeting where certain persons [black and copper color] were."[26] But this is not how it is to be in holiness churches. For the sanctified do "love black and white, Dutch and Italian? If your love is perfected, you love them and can't help it."[27]

A dramatic example of the embodiment of sanctified unity ecclesiology existed in the multiethnic leadership found throughout the radical Holiness movement. George A. Goings, as one outstanding case, rose to top leadership positions in the predominantly white Southern California and Arizona Holiness Association (SCAHA). A part of the SCAHA almost from its inception, Goings and his wife Laura, demonstrated their desire to spread the holiness message through street corner evangelism, prison visits and missionary work to the South. Frank Hall, himself a future participant in the Holiness association, testified to the role the Goings' played in his introduction to the saints:

> I first met the Holiness people in 1891, where, for the first time in my life, I was convicted of sin and felt the need of righteousness through Jesus Christ and saw a way of escape. . . . What first interested me was the singing of a colored man and woman on the street at San Bernardino. I learned afterward it was Bro. and Sister George Goings. They invited us to an upper room around the corner from where they were singing.[28]

Goings tells us that he first received the call to take the holiness message to the South in 1887, but that it was not until 1895 that the urgency of the matter moved him to action. The Goingses left for Kentucky in 1897, where a prosperous ministry among southern blacks commenced. Ultimately, they established their headquarters in Nashville, Tennessee, where George Goings was made chief elder of the Nashville District of the Holiness Church.[29] During their years of work in Nashville, and the surrounding states, they partnered with leading black and white Holiness workers, including J. O.

---

24. George Cole, "National Prejudice," *Gospel Trumpet* 18 no. 48 (December 1, 1898): 1.

25. Martin Wells Knapp, "Unity of Believers," *God's Revivalist*, 12, no. 28 (July 12, 1900): 12.

26. Ibid., 15.

27. Ibid., 12.

28. Washburn, *History and Reminiscences*, 138.

29. *Southern Pentecost* no. 677 (November 23, 1911): 21.

McClurkan, C. P. Jones[30], Joanna P. Moore[31] and J. T. Brown.[32]   In 1909, when President George M. Teel of the Southern California and Arizona Holiness Association arrived in Nashville to evaluate the southern Holiness work among blacks and to assess the value of expanding the Association's work among whites,[33] Goings revealed his close ties to McClurkan by arranging for Teel to stay at the Pentecostal Tabernacle.[34]   Indeed, Teel held Goings, along with his assistant William A. Washington, in such high regard and was so impressed with their work that when the time came to send a white couple as missionaries to the South he asked for their personal ap-

---

30. According the October 30, 1902 issue of the *Zion Outlook*, C. P. Jones addressed the Pentecostal Mission convention in song and sermon and reported that the work of the mission "among the colored people was encouraging." See John T. Benson, *A History 1898-1915 of the Pentecostal Mission, Inc. Nashville, Tennessee* (Nashville, Tenn.: Trevecca Press, 1977), 47.

31. Joanna P. Moore, white evangelist and educator, was influential in bringing C. P. Jones into the experience of sanctification.   Well known for her work in educating African Americans after the Civil War, she was not above using the positive gospel responses of the oppressed to chastise whites who had not made a similar commitment.   In an article entitled "A Plea for More Bible Study," for example, she compared the response of a white man to a Native American after hearing the compelling message of the gospel.   In her story the Native American explained the discrepancy this way: "There comes a rich prince who proposes to give you a new coat. You look at your coat and say: 'I don't know, my coat pretty good: I think it will do a little longer.' He then offers me a new coat. I look at my old blanket; it is good for nothing, and I fling it right away, and accept the new coat. Just so in regard to religion, you looked for a long time at your self-righteousness, and thought it was good enough; but poor Indian had none, and that is the reason I accepted it quickly." Joanna P. Moore, "A Plea for More Bible Study," *Zion's Outlook* 11, no. 8 (February 21, 1901): 7.

32. J. O. McClurkan, "Editorial," *Zion's Outlook* (May 2, 1901): 8; Sister Goings, "From Sister Goings," *The Pentecost* no. 396 (June 26, 1902): 3; Washburn, *History and Reminiscences*, 87-89.

33. Even though the Goings' work primarily targeted the African-American population, they did not hesitate to reach out to whites who were interested in the holiness message.   The *Southern Pentecost* reports that a revival in Providence, Kentucky added thirty to the church and claimed forty experiences of sanctification in meetings "largely attended by both white and colored." *Southern Pentecost*, no. 677 (November 23, 1911): 10.

34. Washburn, *History and Reminiscences*, 429.

proval of the couple before he sent them out.[35] In 1909 he also became one of four elders for the entire Association, the other three being white.[36]

Dependent on SCAHA for financial support, both Goings and his wife often submitted reports in the SCAHA's periodical, *The Pentecost*, working hard to keep the west coast members of the Association informed of their work in the South.[37] As the Southern work grew, the couple began to publish a supplemental paper called the *Southern Pentecost*, which was inserted in each issue of *The Pentecost*.[38] Frequent travelers, the Goings made their way back to Southern California often and were featured speakers at revivals and during SCAHA conventions. The platforms and pulpits of SCAHA churches frequently welcomed women and ethnic minority speakers. Even though the churches established in the South never experienced the same kind of social freedom as the churches in California, the evidence indicates that SCAHA evangelists brought with them the ethos of sanctified unity ecclesiology and implemented it to the extent that they could.

Under Benjamin Irwin's leadership, the Fire-Baptized Holiness Church also became a biracial church. Irwin boldly proclaimed that his experience of sanctification allowed him a new freedom of fellowship at the communion table. No longer bound to his "old hard-shell Baptist" theology, he now easily crossed denominational lines as well as the "color line" when participating in the Lord's Supper. For him the Church of God was now one, all-inclusive family. "I am going to eat with the family. I will commune with you whether you are black or white, yellow or striped. That is because there is unity of the Spirit and unity of the faith in my heart."[39]

Vinson Synan notes that in the first decade of its existence a high degree of interracialism occurred in the Fire-Baptized Holiness Church. Although the church was officially divided between white and "colored" works, a great deal of racial cooperation and mixing characterized its ethos.[40] Isaac

---

35. Washburn, *History and Reminiscences*, 460. "Workers for the South among the white people were raised up in answer to prayers, in the persons of Bro. I. H. and Eva Creswell and little Paul. . . . After consulting Bros. Goings and Washington, we found them of the same opinion, and Bro. and Sister Creswell feeling the call upon them, although they wanted to be very sure."

36. Ibid., 433.

37. There are relatively few issues of *The Pentecost* that do not feature one or more articles by the couple. The subjects range from field reports to sermon topics and even an article on personal finances.

38. The first issue appeared on September 7, 1911.

39. Benjamin Irwin, "The Pentecostal Church," *Live Coals of Fire* (Lincoln, Nebraska) 1, no. 20 (June 1, 1900): 2-3.

40. "Contrary to the growing trend toward total segregation in the 1890s the F.B.H. Church admitted blacks with full equality. They attended integrated churches and conventions. . . . From 1898 to 1908 the Fire-Baptized Church was a striking exam-

Gamble[41] and Uncle Powell Woodbury were noted black evangelists and Alice M. McNeil[42] was an elder in the colored branch.[43]

Irwin worked closely with Gamble. Irwin tells us of a revival that took place in South Carolina in 1899. Gamble, a white saint named James Epps, and Irwin conducted a racially mixed camp meeting. The excellent reputation of both Gamble and Epps, along with respecting southern mores about segregated seating, seems to have prevented any adverse reaction from the local population.[44] Epps, who had six to eight African-American families working for him, was also known for attending his employees' prayer meetings. As Irwin noted in his editorial, he "attends their prayer meetings and thinks it not beneath his dignity to worship God with his colored saints." It is unlikely that the readers of the periodical would have missed Irwin's point about the unifying effects of entire sanctification. But in case they did, Irwin based the revival's success not on the number of people who experienced salvation, sanctification and the power of "dynamite," but instead emphasized its unity, since "everything went on harmoniously."[45]

The outstanding leader to emerge among African Americans in the Fire Baptized Holiness Church was William E. Fuller. Converted in 1897 during a revival in South Carolina, two years later Fuller experienced the "dynamite" under Irwin's preaching. After hearing Irwin speak on the "dynamite," he "went forward and knelt at the altar for it, and God opened up heaven and poured the power down on me."[46] From 1897 to 1900 Fuller

---

ple of interracial worship and accord in the South." Vinson Synan, *The Old-Time Power*, 100.

41. African-American evangelist Isaac Gamble often preached to racially mixed audiences. He reports that during one meeting when several were saved and sanctified "the leading white people of the community came out and showed much interest." Isaac Gamble, "Memoir of Isaac Gamble Colored Evangelist," *Live Coals of Fire* 1, no. 21 (June 15, 1900): 4.

42. McNeill also writes about her experiences in preaching to racially mixed audiences. "Preached in the grove to quite a number of whites and my own color. . . . Have had the best wishes of both white and colored." Alice McNeill, "Alice McNeill's Letter," *Live Coals of Fire* 1, no. 6 (November 10, 1899), 1.

43. "Official List of the Fire-Baptized Holiness Association of America," *Live Coals of Fire* 1, no. 1 (October 6, 1899): 8.

44. "Bro. Gamble was born and raised in this place and his life has been a standing proof of the reality of the doctrine and experience of entire sanctification. Everyone concedes that he is a sanctified man that for thirty years he has lived a holy life; and the same is true of Brother Epps." Benjamin Irwin, "Editorial," *Live Coals of Fire* (Lincoln, Nebraska) 1, no. 5 (November 3, 1899): 1.

45. Ibid., 1. The spiritual experience of the "dynamite" was one of the distinguishing doctrines of the Fire-Baptized Holiness Church. Irwin taught that subsequent to entire sanctification the believer could acquire a third blessing of "fire," a fourth blessing called the "dynamite," and still more blessings of spiritual power after that.

planted over fifty churches for the Holiness group. Five years later, in 1905, he was raised to one of four members who sat on the executive board, the highest office of authority within the Fire-Baptized Holiness Church.[47] The interracial period came to end in 1908 at the request of Fuller. Frustrated by the criticism leveled at the interracial holiness group and the refusal on the part of racist whites to rent buildings to them for integrated revival meetings, Fuller was left with no option but to seek independence from his white brothers and sisters.

African-American evangelists and leaders also played a significant role in the expansion of the Church of God and Reformation Movement. In 1886 the first Church of God Reformation Movement congregation to be headed by an African American was located in Charleston, South Carolina. It was founded and headed by Jane Williams, who worked tirelessly to spread the holiness message throughout the South.[48] She often wrote back to the *Gospel Trumpet* reporting on her evangelistic work. Her commitment to sanctified unity ecclesiology was evident as she crossed racial lines to bring the eradicating power of sanctification into the lives of whites. Her basic optimism in the message of holiness was quite evident, as can be seen in the opening lines of a field report published in 1895, "Dear Saints of God: To-day finds me saved and sanctified through the truth, and also praising dear heavenly Father for the mighty healing power."[49]

The expansion of the Church of God Reformation Movement among Germans and Norwegians in Western Canada includes the improbable story of the African-American evangelist William H. Smith. In a letter published in the *Gospel Trumpet*, October 7, 1909, Smith related how God called him to Edmonton, Canada. "I came here April 28, 1906 as God had made it plain to me before leaving the States that I should come here and preach the gospel on the streets and from house to house and distribute Trumpets and tracts in English, German, and Norwegian." In September of 1907 evangelist William Ebel joined Smith in Edmonton for a revival. Ebel reports that some of the participants "came by wagon one hundred and twenty miles, others quite a distance by railroad." Smith also successfully reached out to a not inconsiderable number of African-American settlers east and northeast of Edmonton. By the end of 1907, the positive response to the gospel message

---

46. Synan, *The Old-Time Power*, 100; William E. Fuller, "W. E. Fuller's (Colored) Letter," *Live Coals of Fire* (Lincoln, Nebraska) 1, no.2 (January 26, 1900): 1.

47. Synan, *The Old-Time Power*, 100. Synan also records that Fuller served as trustee for the church.

48. David A. Telfer, *Red and Yellow Black and White and Brown: Home Missions in the Church of God* (Anderson, Ind.: Warner Press, 1981), 46; James Earl Massey, *An Introduction to the Negro Churches in the Church of God Reformation Movement*, 19.

49. Jane Williams, "News from the Field," *Gospel Trumpet* (Grand Junction, Mich.) 15, no. 45 (November 14, 1895): 4.

allowed Smith to establish the "Gospel Mission to All Nations," in all proba-
bility the first Church of God in Western Canada.[50]

Conclusion

The degree to which whites, blacks and browns interacted with each other
in the radical Holiness movement has not been fully appreciated. As this
brief survey demonstrates, different racial and ethnic groups fully participated together in the work of leadership, fellowship and the evangelistic
activities of sanctified unity churches. From preaching in the pulpit at camp
meetings and on the streets to working alongside seekers in the midst of
revival, blacks and browns shared an equal status with their white brothers
and sisters that had never been experienced before in the American church.
The numerous field reports in radical holiness journals that came from racial and ethnic minorities confirms the tremendous amount of energy that
they invested in the spread of the holiness message. It also reveals that the
mostly white editorial staff responsible for the publication and distribution
of the periodicals was equally convinced of the sanctified unity ecclesiology
message that gripped their brown and black brothers and sisters. No sense
of favoritism can be detected in who was published and who was not. Holiness papers existed to pass on the excitement of the present movement of
God. Any word of God's miraculous activities in these last days was welcome no matter the source. Indeed, that the source was often someone
from one of the disenfranchised peoples of the nation in and of itself was a
demonstration of God's plan to restore the Church of God to its original unity.

The egalitarian result of sanctified unity ecclesiology would not be lim-
ited to radical holiness churches. With the spread of Pentecostalism from a
regional movement into an international one at the Azusa Street revival,
sanctified unity ecclesiology extended its influence into another church
movement. The next chapter details how sanctified unity theology permeated the thinking of the leadership and first participants at the Apostolic
Faith Mission in Los Angeles and created a church environment open to the
mixing of racial and ethnic groups.

---

50. "Gospel Mission to All Nations" strongly suggests the interracial and multiethnic
characteristics of this body of saints. Douglas E. Welch, "Jottings from the Archives,"
Church of God Historian 4 no. 1 (Fall 2003): 6-7.

Chapter Five

Sanctified Unity Ecclesiology and
The Azusa Street Revival

From 1906 to 1909 radical holiness folk flowed into Los Angeles from every corner of the United States seeking the pentecostal experience of Spirit baptism. The humble city surroundings of the Azusa Street Mission belied the great eschatological expectations the seekers brought with them to southern California. Renamed the "American Jerusalem" by Frank Bartleman, events now occurring in Los Angeles were believed to be the final outpouring of the Holy Spirit to usher in the last days and the soon return of Christ.

Holiness radicals did not bring to the revival their expectations only, but also their distinctive Wesleyan theological beliefs and church experiences. What made these adherents to radical Wesleyan holiness unusual was their core conviction that the experience of sanctification should lead to one corporate church, and unity should follow across racial, gender and social barriers. At the helm of the revival was William J. Seymour, an African-American preacher who had imbibed the movement's theological ideas from some of its best teachers. Not just a placid follower of radical holiness doctrine Seymour also nuanced and prioritized key concepts to create a revival event never seen before in the United States.

Looking back historians of early Pentecostalism have emphasized the role of "speaking in tongues" in Spirit baptism as key to understanding the new religious movement, and with good cause. A core doctrine within the emerging pentecostal sect its very uniqueness in the American religious experience set it apart as something *sui generis*. Perusing the work of pentecostal historians from both inside and outside the movement, most have arrived at the same principal conclusion: it was the work of Spirit baptism which created a transgressive space for all "nationalities" to meet and interact with one another in an atmosphere of racial acceptance and equality. Early pentecostal belief held *xenolalia*, or "speaking a foreign tongue," was the "Bible evidence" of the Baptism of the Holy Spirit. This meant for the first pentecostals that the Spirit was accelerating the process of world evangelization for the soon return of Jesus Christ. Later generations of pentecostals connected the eschatological outpouring of the Spirit with the unity that prevailed at Azusa.[1] A casual reading of *The Apostolic Faith* paper, moreover, reveals that the revivalists themselves gave credit to the work of Spirit baptism in breaking down the barriers of race, along with gender and social class. This view crossed over into the academy and was further developed with the publications of Robert Mapes Anderson's social history of Pentecostalism in 1979, *Vision of the Disinherited: The Making of American Pentecostalism* and, in 1981, Douglas J. Nelson's more theologically-oriented dissertation on William J. Seymour, "For Such a Time as This: The Story of Bishop William J. Seymour and the Azusa Street Revival."[2] Seventy-five years after the pentecostal outburst at Azusa Street, the work of these, and other, professional historians put into academic language what popular Pentecostalism had always held: "Speaking in tongues also constituted a common Pentecostal 'language,' bridging the gaps between the many accents, dialect, and languages of the Pentecostals, and providing a 'linguistic' basis for a new community of the Spirit."[3]

This chapter will challenge and seek to nuance the dominant historiographical position that has developed within academic circles over the last thirty years. As outlined in the introduction, I will argue that sanctified unity ecclesiology explains more completely the language and theological constructions used by the leadership and participants to call for corporate and communal unity during the Azusa Street revival. More specifically, this chapter will demonstrate that the radical holiness doctrine of sanctified unity was responsible primarily for the practice of multiethnic worship, noted by most as one of the great hallmarks of the revival in Los Angeles.

The Azusa Street Revival

The history of the Azusa Street revival is reflected in no better sources than the revival's periodical, *The Apostolic Faith*, personal testimonies and early histories. It is within the pages of *The Apostolic Faith*, however, that the Wesleyan holiness theological matrix of sanctified unity ecclesiology is clearly presented in statements, testimonials, field reports and articles. It is also here that the new pentecostal experience of Spirit-baptism is integrated into radical holiness theology. Whereas within radical holiness circles the Spirit moved through sanctification alone to create unity within the

---

1. Carl Brumback, *A Sound from Heaven* (Springfield, Mo.: Gospel Publishing House, 1977), 82; Jacobsen, *Thinking in the Spirit*, 267.
2. Robert Mapes Anderson, *Vision of the Disinherited: The Making of American Pentecostalism* (New York: Oxford University Press, 1979); Douglas J. Nelson, "For Such a Time as This: The Story of Bishop William J. Seymour and the Azusa Street Revival" (diss., University of Birmingham [U.K.], 1981).
3. Anderson, *Vision of the Disinherited*, 235.

body of Christ, now the third experience of Spirit baptism was given a role in achieving oneness in the church. Nevertheless, at the Azusa Street revival entire sanctification was still the primary initiator of sanctified unity. Therefore, keeping radical holiness theology in view as the Azusa Street revival progressed is critical to understanding the ecclesiology of racial and ethnic unity as presented in *The Apostolic Faith.*

Restorationist Eschatology:
"The Old-Time Apostolic Assembly"

The participants of the Azusa Street revival were convinced restorationists. Similar to their radical holiness brothers and sisters, they sought the life and experience of the New Testament church. They longed to erase the accretions of church creeds and traditions and be rebaptized in the unpolluted waters of the first century church. They were of firm conviction that God had been restoring biblical Christianity since the time of Luther. There appeared in the October, 1906 edition of *The Apostolic Faith* periodical the same "'progressive' restorationist historiography"[4] found in the Holiness movement:

> All along the ages men have been preaching a partial Gospel. A part of the Gospel remained when the world went into the dark ages. God has from time to time raised up men to bring back the truth to the church. He raised up Luther to bring back to the world the doctrine of justification of faith. He raised up another reformer in John Wesley to establish Bible holiness in the church. Then he raised up Dr. Cullis who brought back to the world the wonderful doctrine of divine healing. Now He is bringing back the Pentecostal Baptism to the church.[5]

Participants at Azusa Street believed "Pentecostal Baptism" was the last in a line of restored New Testament practices. Florence Crawford captured the excitement of the theology and the experience, writing in 1907, "O to think we have lived to see the return of the apostolic power and to see gifts restored to the church."[6] The leadership at the Apostolic Faith Mission, as well, defined the organization of the saints gathered at Azusa in restorationist terms, "It is the old-time apostolic assembly, the same old teaching of 1900 years ago. It is new to the world in these last days, but its teaching and doctrine is old as the New Testament."[7] Finally, the statement of faith of the Apostolic Faith Mission given in the first issue of the periodical left no

---

4. Joe Creech, "Visions of Glory: The Place of the Azusa Street Revival in Pentecostal History," *Church History* 65 (1996): 419.

5. "The Pentecostal Baptism Restored: The Promised Latter Rain Now Being Poured Out on God's Humble People," *The Apostolic Faith* (Los Angeles) (October 1906): 1.

6. Florence Crawford, *AF* (Los Angeles) (June to September 1907): 4.

7. *The Apostolic Faith* (October to January 1908): 2.

doubt as to the overall pentecostal view, claiming that the movement, "Stands for the restoration of the faith once delivered unto the saints."[8]

Of all the revelations that pentecostals received during these early days the least surprising prophecy was that proclaiming the spiritual outpouring at Azusa Street as the restoration of New Testament power and practice in their day. One of the most alluded to and oft quoted verses used among the ranks of the radical holiness folk, Heb 13:8, states that God is "just the same today," or more precisely, "He is the same yesterday, today, and forever."[9] The first pentecostals interpreted their experiences as equal to the miraculous events they read about in their Bibles. The phrase "this is that" became common currency within pentecostal circles.[10] These were the words that Peter had spoken to describe the first Pentecost as the fulfillment of the prophecy of Joel 2. Pentecostals adopted the same expression to explain the eschatological events that were taking place during their day.

The Azusa Street believers were advocates of the "latter rain" and "evening light" eschatologies, first propagated within radical holiness circles. At Pentecost God first poured out the "early rain," but now, in these last days before the return of Christ, God was opening the skies for the "latter rain." If the former rain had been moderately given, the "latter rain" would be poured out in greater measure upon his people. Equally, "when the Holy Ghost fell on the one hundred and twenty it was in the morning of the dispensation of the Holy Ghost. Today we are living down in the evening of the dispensation of the Holy Ghost."[11] The reason for this was simple, "there are greater things to be done in these last days of the Holy Ghost."[12] This proposition was confirmed by the arrival of field reports concerning God's activities within their own nation and around the world. The Spirit-baptized saints were ecstatic to hear that other nations were experiencing the same Pentecost and interpreted it through their own eschatological prism: "Truly, these are marvelous days. Reports are coming in from nearly every quarter of the globe of how the latter rain is falling in many places and, truly, it is encouraging to see that the God of Pentecost is just the same today."[13] Or similarly, "How wonderful it is that today in different parts of India, Russia, Norway, Sweden, England, Canada, Africa and America, God's

---

8. "The Apostolic Faith Mission," *The Apostolic Faith* (Los Angeles) (January 1908): 2.

9. William J. Seymour, "Letter To One Seeking the Holy Ghost," *AF* (Los Angeles) (June to September 1907): 3.

10. William J. Seymour, "River of Living Water," *AF* (Los Angeles) (November 1906): 2; A. H. Post, "Testimony of a Minister," *AF* (Los Angeles) (January 1907): 4; Florence Crawford, "A Cheering Testimony," *AF* (Los Angeles) (October to January 1908): 4.

11. "This Same Jesus," *The Apostolic Faith* (Los Angeles) (October 1906): 3.

12. *The Apostolic Faith* (Los Angeles) (September 1906): 4.

13. A. H. Argue, "Italians and Indians Receive the Holy Ghost," *AF* (Los Angeles) (May 1908): 4.

saints are enjoying the latter rain and are being satisfied."[14] The "greater things to be done," then, was the final mission to the world. But even as they spread the gospel around the globe the faithful at Azusa continued to look expectantly towards the heavens. The long hoped for return of Christ awaited the completion of world evangelization.

Christ's soon return also provided an explanation for the final outpouring of God's Spirit to empower the saints to take the good news to the ends of the earth. From the pages of *The Apostolic Faith* they declared that "this is a world-wide revival, the last Pentecostal revival to bring our Jesus. The church is taking her last march to meet her beloved."[15] Prophecies and interpretation of tongues abounded to this effect, confirming the near return of the Lord: "Jesus is coming again, Coming again so soon, And we shall meet Him then. Prepare your hearts now, for the Lord is coming soon, and ye know not the hour. . . ."[16] One report came in from Winnipeg, Canada, relating the experience of some recent Native American converts, "While the Indians were at the meetings in the city, two of the saints, under the power of the Spirit, spoke in other languages, which were understood by the Indians and one of the interpretations was, 'Jesus is coming soon.'"[17] For William Seymour the experience was palpable, "O, I feel the coming of our Lord and Savious [sic] Jesus Christ drawing nigh."[18]

Yet world evangelization was not the only critical preparation to be considered in readying the church for the Parousia. The writings in *The Apostolic Faith* demonstrate that the ecclesiological doctrine of sanctified unity had thoroughly permeated the eschatology of the first pentecostals. As A. H. Post wrote in *The Way of Faith*, and republished in the Azusa periodical, the "latter rain" was being poured "out upon all flesh" and "God's children [are] one, and the coming of Jesus intensely real."[19] Moreover, Christ's return was to be for his bride. Seymour wrote, "now we are living in the eventide of this dispensation, when the Holy Spirit is leading us, Christ's bride, to meet Him in the clouds."[20]

The radical holiness eschatology preached in the Apostolic Faith Mission taught that the bride of Christ must be literally "without spot or wrinkle." What did this mean exactly for Seymour and the Azusa Street faithful? At

---

14. "From Distant Lands," *The Apostolic Faith*, (Los Angeles) (June to September 1907): 1.

15. *The Apostolic Faith* (Los Angeles) (September 1906): 4.

16 ."A Message Concerning His Coming," *The Apostolic Faith* (Los Angeles) (October 1906): 3.

17. A. H. Argue, "Italians and Indians Receive the Holy Ghost," *AF* (Los Angeles) (May 1908): 4.

18. William J. Seymour, "Testimony and Praise to God," *AF* (Los Angeles) (June to September 1907): 4.

19. A. H. Post, "Testimony of a Minister," *AF* (Los Angeles) (January 1907): 4.

20. William J. Seymour, "Rebecca: Type of the Bride of Christ-Gen. 24," *AF* (Los Angeles) (February-March 1907): 2.

its core it meant recapturing the sanctified unity of the New Testament church. "The Lord Jesus wants a church, when He comes back to earth, just like the one He started when He left the earth and organized it on the day of Pentecost. . . ."[21] In short, Jesus' high priestly prayer was to be fulfilled so "that all may be one," corporately and communally. The Apostolic Faith leadership at Azusa Street stated best this second condition for the Lord's coming in the February-March, 1907 issue of the *The Apostolic Faith*, "One token of the Lord's coming is that He is melting all races and nations together, and they are filled with the power and glory of God. He is baptizing by one spirit into one body and making up a people that will be ready to meet Him when He comes."[22] Later that same year the connection between the last days, world evangelization, sanctified unity and the Lord's coming was made even more cogently in an untitled and unsigned piece:

> The Lord wants a people in these days that will make the very highest consecration to God. He wants us to step up to the heights of holiness. We are in a time when we ought to be looking for the greatest revival the world had ever had, because the time is drawing nigh when the Scripture says, "And He shall send Jesus Christ. . . ." Now, beloved, if we come together in unity and love and look to God, He can send an earthquake to this old world. . . .[23]

Thus, one aim of the nascent Pentecostal movement's eschatological restorationism was to establish an ecclesiology of sanctified unity. The Lord's soon arrival for his bride demanded both the evangelization of the world and a bride suitable for the wedding feast in heaven. For those who were part of the radical holiness milieu, Jesus' high priestly prayer in John 17 was the standard by which to judge her readiness. This meant that the church needed to practice complete unity of body, corporately and communally. All peoples were to be brought together in unity in one Church of God.

But if this was the necessary goal, the *telos* of radical holiness theology, what was the means? The first pentecostals sought to integrate their new experience of Spirit baptism into the radical holiness ecclesiology of sanctified unity and the concomitant role of the second blessing. The interplay of entire sanctification and the baptism of the Holy Spirit together would provide the catalyst needed to prepare the bride of Christ for his return.

Entire Sanctification:
"What God Has Wrought Within You"

During the Azusa Street revival participants were exhorted to cleanse the heart of all carnality as preparation for the baptism of the Holy Spirit. Justi-

---

21. William J. Seymour, "The Baptism of the Holy Ghost," *AF* (Los Angeles) (May 1908): 3.
22. *The Apostolic Faith* (Los Angeles) (February-March 1907): 7.
23. *The Apostolic Faith* (Los Angeles) (October to January 1908): 4.

fication, following Wesleyan teaching, removed from the believer's life the sin which he had committed. Yet deeper in the life of the justified person still existed a depraved nature passed down through the generations from the time of Adam. Moreover, the sinful nature frustrated the believer's ability to live in holiness. All Wesleyans understood Heb 12:14, "Without holiness no one can see the Lord," to mean that Christians must be righteous in their actual being and not simply declared righteous as the Protestant reformers had taught. "Before you can receive the baptism of the Holy Ghost, you must have a thorough definite experience of justification and sanctification. . . . First, what God has done for you, second, what God had wrought within you."[24] Within holiness theology, as a result, entire sanctification became the means to acquire actual righteousness. It was believed at Azusa that the purity of the human vessel was essential to a proper reception of Spirit baptism. Entire sanctification, then, was viewed as paramount to a correct reception of the baptism of the Holy Spirit.

Phoebe Palmer's "altar theology" was the standard theology of sanctification preached at the Apostolic Faith Mission. Altar theology taught that the justified person must place his soul upon the altar for Jesus to cleanse. William Seymour explained the second work,

> there is Jesus, the Lamb without blemish, on the altar. Jesus takes that soul that has eternal life in it and presents it to God for thorough purging and cleansing from all original and Adamic sin. And Jesus, the Son of God, cleanse him from all sin, and he is made every whit whole, sanctified and holy.[25]

During the Azusa Street revival the role of Jesus received priority over the Holy Spirit in sanctification. In the first light of the Pentecostal movement there was some confusion over whom to give credit for the second grace of sanctification. In the late nineteenth century a *modus vivendi* had been reached between Wesleyan and Reformed believers in the Holiness movement over the issue of sanctification. Both agreed to set aside their doctrinal differences and refer to it as a "baptism in the Holy Spirit."[26] When Charles Parham formulated a third experience, different in purpose to sanctification, and labeled the experience the "baptism of the Holy Spirit" with the Bible evidence of speaking in tongues, the theological situation became more complex. Under Parham's instruction no longer could there be a compromise over the description of sanctification between the Wesleyan and Reformed faithful. As a result a three-staged approach was developed along Wesleyan lines. But if sanctification was not the baptism of

---

24. *The Apostolic Faith* (Los Angeles) (April 1907): 3.
25. William J. Seymour, "The Way into the Holies," *AF* (Los Angeles) (October 1906): 4.
26. See Dieter, Holiness Revival, 15-128; Dayton, *Theological Roots of Pentecostalism*, 87-114.

the Holy Spirit, what was it? The saints at Azusa were still wrestling with this problem five years later. In their descriptions of the work of sanctification both Jesus and the Holy Spirit are given credit. However, it is always the "blood of Jesus" which is given priority over the work of the Spirit. The central role of the Spirit is relegated to the baptism of the Holy Spirit.

The role of the blood of Jesus in the second work of sanctification was prominent within radical holiness teaching. Seymour and the leaders of the Azusa Street revival adopted the centrality of Jesus' blood for their own explanation of sanctification. In an unsigned article entitled "The Golden Altar, Sanctification," imagery from the Jewish temple is used as an analogy to understand the three-staged event of justification, sanctification and Spirit baptism. The blood of Jesus is critical for the first two stages of grace which prepares the believer for the third phase of Spirit baptism.

"There are two altars, the brazen altar and the golden altar. We see this represents two works of grace, two altars. Now the believer comes to the golden altar. Since the new birth is implanted in his soul, he has access to present himself a living offering. When he came as a sinner, he was dead in trespasses and sins, and had nothing to consecrate. Now he can consecrate himself to be sanctified. Here he finds on the altar the Blood of Jesus, which represents Christ the sanctifier of His people. He receives Christ to rule and reign supreme in his soul, and every enemy of doubt and carnality is cast out and destroyed by the Blood. Then he is one with Christ. For both He that sanctifieth and they who are sanctified are all of one . . . The only way men and women can be preserved is by living on the altar . . . Then you are prepared for the baptism with the Holy Ghost."[27]

The recognition of the blood of Jesus for sanctification is ubiquitous in the writings of *The Apostolic Faith*. This is especially true in the writings of William Seymour. In the first issue of the Azusa Street periodical in September 1906, he wrote that "we receive sanctification through the blood of Jesus."[28] In response to the question "Does a soul need the baptism with the Holy Ghost in order to live a pure and holy life?" in the question and answer section of the October to January 1908 issue, Seymour and the leadership responded, "It is the blood that cleanses and makes holy, and through the Blood we receive the baptism of the Holy Spirit. The Holy Ghost always falls in answer to the Blood."[29] At times it caused him to exult in the Lord, "How

---

27. "The Golden Altar, Sanctification," *The Apostolic Faith* (Los Angeles) (September 1907): 3. See B. Scott Lewis' article "William J. Seymour: Follower of the 'Evening Light' (Zech. 14:7)," *Wesleyan Theological Journal* 39, no. 2 (Fall 2004), for a convincing argument for the further influence of the Church of God (Anderson) on Seymour's theology of holiness.

28. William J. Seymour, "The Precious Atonement," *AF* (Los Angeles) (September 1906): 2.

29. *The Apostolic Faith* (Los Angeles) (October to January 1908): 2.

I worship Him today! How I praise Him for the all-cleansing blood!"[30] The importance of the blood of Jesus as a theological concept is critical to understanding Seymour's explanation of sanctified unity.

Sanctified Unity: "One church, one holy body"

William J. Seymour's argument for the central role of sanctification in the pentecostal experience provided him a platform from which to propagate an interracial and multiethnic biblical ecclesiology. The main role of the Spirit in Seymour's pentecostal theology was to empower the believer to take the message of God's "full gospel" to the world. But at the forefront of the "full gospel" message was the experience of entire sanctification. "How true it is in this day, when we get the baptism with the Holy Spirit, we have something to tell, and it is that the blood of Jesus Christ cleanseth from all sins."[31] For Seymour, entire sanctification created the possibility for sanctified unity fellowship. Corporately, through the sanctifying blood of Jesus, the church is structurally one and no longer separated by denominationalism. Equally, the church is communally one, no longer divided along racial and ethnic lines. The Spirit will act as a complement to the blood of Jesus to establish sanctified unity within the church, but primarily it will energize the spread of the biblical message of sanctified unity ecclesiology in anticipation of the Lord's Second Coming.

First, then, it is important to understand the role of sanctification in the restoration of the New Testament church in the theology of Seymour and his co-participants at Azusa Street. The critical years of the Azusa Street revival, 1906 - 1909, bear the marks of radical Wesleyan holiness. With Seymour as its leader the early Pentecostal movement never strayed from its commitment to holiness doctrine. Indeed, under his guiding hand minor doctrinal aspects of radical holiness theology, namely interracial and multiethnic fellowship as understood within sanctified unity, were purposely brought to the forefront and made a mandatory part of the fruit of the "full gospel." The two aspects of sanctified unity ecclesiology taught within radical holiness-the restoration of the New Testament "Church of God" and a radical egalitarianism cutting across the boundaries of race, gender and class-were both present at Azusa Street. As with most aspects of the holiness teaching he received, Seymour nuanced each doctrine and turned it to his purpose of racial oneness. In light of this, Seymour and many of his fellow pentecostal compatriots at Azusa should be viewed as innovators as well as followers of radical holiness theology. Therefore, what is only nascent in radical holiness circles, both in theological reflection and in practice, is more fully developed in the early years of the Azusa Street revival.

---

30. William J. Seymour, "River of Living Water," *AF* (Los Angeles) (November 1906): 2.
31. William J. Seymour, "River of Living Water," *AF* (Los Angeles) (November 1906): 2.

Like their brothers and sisters in the radical wing of the Holiness movement, the first pentecostals believed that true corporate unity could occur
only with a return to the original *ecclesia*. The participants at Azusa Street
were instinctively anti-denominational. For the Spirit-baptized saints, man-
made denominations were the clearest expression of humanity's innate
selfishness. In their view the fulfillment of Jesus' high priestly prayer could
never be achieved through the Protestant churches. Mrs. Anna Hall put it
succinctly, "What is the matter with the world today? Here is a little selfish
sect and there a denomination by itself. They do not love one another as
God would have them."[32] As a result, in the minds of the early pentecostals
ecclesiological unity was possible only through a return to the original
Church of God, or more precisely for the saints in Los Angeles, the "Apostolic Faith." As the editors of *The Apostolic Faith* proclaimed in the first issue,
"the Pentecostal movement is too large to be confined in any denomination
or sect. It works outside, drawing all together in one bond of love, one
church, one body of Christ."[33] Over a year later they were voicing the same
sentiment. Under the question, "Is this movement a new sect or denomination?" in a question and answer section, they emphatically responded, "No;
it is undenominational and unsectarian. We believe in unity with Christ's
people everywhere, in the Word of God. It is the old-time apostolic assembly...."[34]

Moreover, the restoration of the true *ecclesia* must be visible. Once
again, living out the theology they had learned in radical holiness circles,
the participants at Azusa believed the invisible church of traditional
Protestant theology must be made visible. Because of their Wesleyan theological presupposition that holiness was the *sine qua non* of the faith, they
could not tolerate the notion of a mixed church of sinners and saints. For
them the existence of sinners in denominational churches was one of the
hallmarks of denominational apostasy from true biblical faith. The representation of saints and sinners in the same church confirmed the notion
that genuine unity could never exist in "denominational sects." The pentecostal mission's claim to "apostolic faith" was demonstrated by its visible
unity. This lent great authority to the faithful residing in the former AME
church on Azusa Street. Hence, William Seymour never hesitated when he
called "all Christ's people and ministers everywhere . . . [to] stop by the
headquarters, the Jerusalem of God, for their credentials. Then they are
entitled to receive credentials from the visible church."[35]

Holiness-Pentecostals believed also that entire sanctification led to a
communal unity within the New Testament church. All ambition was to be

---

32. Anna Hall, "Honor the Holy Ghost," *AF* (Los Angeles) (October 1906): 4.
33. *The Apostolic Faith* (Los Angeles) (September 1906): 1.
34. *The Apostolic Faith* (Los Angeles) (October to January 1908): 2.
35. William J. Seymour, "The Holy Spirit: Bishop of the Church," *AF* (Los Angeles)
(June to September 1907): 3.

crucified through the cleansing blood of Jesus shed on the cross. A favorite scripture verse, Heb 13:12, summed up the sentiments of holiness theology concisely, "wherefore, Jesus also, that He might sanctify the people with His own blood, suffered without the gate." If we are to die to self, Seymour argued, we must let the temptations of the world, "precious temples, fame, honor, position," all found within the "beautiful city" be crucified outside the gate with Christ. [36] In a similar vein Galatians 5:24-25 states, "and they that are Christ's have crucified the flesh, with the affections and lusts." Only then, once the Adamic nature has been removed can the love of the brethren be restored in unity and oneness. As their holiness brothers and sisters had argued before them, this was the long awaited answer to Jesus' high priestly prayer in John 17. Nevertheless, the first pentecostals found it difficult to implement. This is evident in that Seymour still was imploring the faithful to live in sanctified unity with one another in May 1908.

"Apostolic Faith doctrine means one accord, one soul, one heart. May God help every child of His to live in Jesus' prayer. "That they all may be one, as Thou Father, art in Me and I in Thee; that they all may be one in us; that the world may believe that Thou hast sent me." Praise God! O how my heart cries out to God in these days that He would make every child of His see the necessity of living in the 17th chapter of John, that we may be one in the body of Christ, as Jesus has prayed.

When we are sanctified through the truth, then we are one in Christ. . . ."[37]

The Apostolic Faith Mission leadership believed that sanctified unity ecclesiology should be the norm among the saints. Much like their holiness forebears, they were fond of quoting 1 John 1:7, which stated that once all sin had been cleansed through the blood of Jesus Christ then true Christian fellowship could begin among the faithful.[38] The pages of *The Apostolic Faith* trumpeted the role of sanctification in the creation of biblical fellowship. One untitled piece exclaimed, "It is the Blood of Jesus that brings fellowship among the Christian family. The Blood of Jesus Christ is the strongest in the world. It makes all races and nations into one common family in the Lord and makes them all satisfied to be one."[39] In case anyone had confused the role of the baptism of the Holy Spirit with the role of sanctification in the restoration of the apostolic faith, in the question and answer section it was asked, "Is the speaking in tongues the standard of fellowship with the Pentecost people?" To this the editors responded unequivocally, "No; our

---

36. William J. Seymour, "Counterfeits," *AF* (Los Angeles) (December 1906): 2.

37. William J. Seymour, "The Baptism of the Holy Ghost," *AF* (Los Angeles) (May 1908): 3.

38. William J. Seymour, "River of Living Water," *AF* (Los Angeles) (November 1906): 2; William J. Seymour, "Counterfeits," *AF* (Los Angeles) (December 1906): 2.

39. *The Apostolic Faith* (Los Angeles) (April 1907): 3.

fellowship does not come through gifts and outward demonstrations but through the Blood by the Spirit of Christ. There is nothing more loving than the Blood of Jesus Christ in our hearts."[40]

In his invaluable work, *How Pentecost Came to Los Angeles: As It Was in the Beginning*, Frank Bartleman, the peripatetic and prolific holiness writer, has given the world the memorable phrase "the 'color line' was washed away in the blood."[41] Many scholars have failed to connect this well-worn phrase to the sanctifying role of the blood of Jesus in radical holiness theology. The effect has been to overlook the role of entire sanctification in breaking down the walls of racial and ethnic division in favor of the work of Spirit baptism. However, Bartleman's emphasis was on the blood's work in sanctification, not Spirit baptism. Reading the famous quote in context demonstrates this more clearly:

> The place was packed out nightly. The whole building, upstairs and down, had now been cleared and put into use. There were far more white people than colored coming. The "color line" was washed away in the blood. A.S. Worrell, translator of the New Testament, declared the "Azusa" work had rediscovered the blood of Christ to the church at that time. Great emphasis was placed on the "blood," for cleansing, etc. A high standard was held up for a clean life.[42]

The Azusa Street revival required a three-staged experience to receive the baptism of the Holy Spirit. A person had to be justified, then sanctified and only then was he or she ready for Spirit baptism. Bartleman's description of the sanctifying work of Jesus' blood is best interpreted in the Wesleyan context of the revival. As such it is strong testimony that the first pentecostals believed in the efficacious nature of entire sanctification to unify the races. One of his holiness tracts, "That They All May Be One," contended for the unity of the body of Christ on the radical holiness basis of John 17.[43] This paralleled his own previous experience of eating, sleeping and working with blacks as an itinerant evangelist in the South. Like George Goings of the Southern California and Arizona Holiness Association, he addressed the plight of African Americans in the South through biting social commentary.

"The white man robbed the negro systematically of what little money he could earn, and seemed to have no conscience in doing so. He considered him lawful prey. A whole town would turn out to lynch a negro. And they were not always too careful to prove him guilty either. Often a white man would black himself up when he wanted to commit a crime. After all I

---

40. *The Apostolic Faith* (Los Angeles) (October to January 1908): 2.
41. Frank Bartleman, "How Pentecost Came to Los Angeles: As It Was in the Beginning," in *Witness to Pentecost: The Life of Frank Bartleman*, ed. Donald Dayton (New York: Garland, 1985).
42. Ibid., 54.
43. Bartleman, "How Pentecost Came to Los Angeles", 26.

found the negro was largely only what circumstances had made him, in the south. He was given little encouragement to do better."[44]

As a participant in the Azusa Street revival, Bartleman experienced firsthand the sanctified unity ecclesiology of the Apostolic Faith Mission. He recorded that he frequented the prayer meetings taking place on Bonnie Brae street prior to its move to Azusa Street. As a part of the radical holiness ethos of sanctified unity, indeed as an advocate of it, Bartleman was well prepared to interpret the events along the same lines as the revival's leadership. As Bartleman considered the developing situation at the little mission building on Azusa street, he concluded that it was the sanctifying blood of Jesus in which the "color line" was washed away.[45]

To complement the sanctified unity ecclesiology taught within the periodical, the editors also included a wide assortment of references to racially and ethnically diverse people active within the nascent Pentecostal movement. The sheer number and diversity demonstrates that the leaders of the Azusa Street revival were conscious of the significance of interracial and multiethnic fellowship and intentional in advertising it to the church. For example, in one account it is the faith of a "poor Mexican Indian" which unleashes God's healing power upon an ailing saint.[46] A revealing description of the Azusa Street meetings appeared in the November 1906 edition of *The Apostolic Faith*, "It is noticeable how free all nationalities feel . . . No instrument that God can use is rejected on account of color or dress or lack of education."[47] The next line revealed the perspective of the writer, "This is why God has so built up the work."[48] The headline for the lead article in the October 1906 issue broadcast, "The Pentecostal Baptism Restored: The

---

44. Frank Bartleman, "From Plow to Pulpit, from Maine to California," in *Witness to Pentecost: The Life of Frank Bartleman*, ed. Donald Dayton (New York: Garland 1985): 42.

45. Bartleman's complete commitment to sanctified unity theology is clearly expressed in his decision to separate from the Azusa Street revival. "Sure enough the very next day after I dropped this warning in the meeting I found a sign outside 'Azusa' reading 'Apostolic Faith Mission.' The Lord said: 'That is what I told you.' They had done it. Surely a 'party spirit' cannot be 'Pentecostal.' There can be no divisions in a true Pentecost. To formulate a separate body is but to advertise our failure, as a people of God. It proves to the world that we cannot get along together, rather than causing them to believe in our salvation. "That they may all be one; that the world may believe." --John 17: 21 . . . Christ is one, and His 'body' can be but 'one.' To divide it is but to destroy it, as with the natural body. 'In one Spirit were we all baptized into one body.'--1 Cor. 12:13." Frank Bartleman, *Witness to Pentecost: The Life of Frank Bartleman*, ed. Donald Dayton (New York: Garland 1985); reprint, *How Pentecost Came to Los Angeles: How It Was in the Beginning* (Los Angeles: n.p., 1925), 68.

46. *The Apostolic Faith* (Los Angeles) (September 1906): 2.

47. *The Apostolic Faith* (Los Angeles) "Bible Pentecost: Gracious Pentecostal Showers Continue to Fall," (November 1906): 1.

48. Ibid., 1.

Promised Latter Rain Now Being Poured out on God's Humble People." The article went on to explain that God "is no respecter of persons and places."[49] Finally, in January 1907 A. H. Post provided a sweeping expression of the egalitarian nature of the services at Azusa Street. "Many of all ages and races, from varied conditions and abilities, from the very young to the octogenarian, those learned, and of no education, each alike has received a definite baptism of the Holy Spirit."[50]

The editors of the periodical also used field reports to substantiate their claim that entire sanctification brought all peoples together in Christian unity. Gaston Barnabas Cashwell sent frequent reports to the leadership at Azusa Street describing the spread of the pentecostal message among holiness groups in the Southeastern section of the United States. His reports demonstrate that along with receiving the baptism of the Holy Spirit during his visit to Azusa Street he also imbibed its interracial ecclesiology. Indeed, if in Frank Bartleman we have a person who reported on the startling events of interracial and multiethnic fellowship at Azusa, then G. B. Cashwell is the sort of changed person about whom Bartleman was writing.

Cashwell was a minister with the Pentecostal Holiness Church of North Carolina, a part of the Wesleyan branch of the Holiness-Pentecostal movement. After reading reports about the pentecostal revival in Los Angeles in his local holiness paper, Cashwell decided to travel to California in late 1906 to experience it firsthand. He did not leave, however, before seeking to restore his life to the proper holiness standard. In a letter to his fellow ministers Cashwell related the start of his sanctifying preparation to receive Spirit baptism:

"If I have offended anyone of you, forgive me. I realize that my life has fallen short of the standard of holiness we preach; but I have repented in my home in Dunn, North Carolina, and I have been restored. I am unable to be with you this time, for I am now leaving for Los Angeles, California, where I shall seek for the Baptism of the Holy Ghost."[51]

On his arrival at Azusa Street Cashwell was immediately impressed that "God was in it."[52] His Southern racial sensibilities were upset, however, when he discovered that blacks were playing an instrumental role in the revival. The problem did not lie in the racially mixed atmosphere at the Apostolic Faith Mission. Cashwell had preached to interracial crowds in the Southeast.[53] What disturbed Cashwell and revealed his deep-seated racism

---

49. "The Pentecostal Baptism Restored: The Promised Latter Rain Now Being Poured out on God's Humble People," *The Apostolic Faith* (Los Angles) (October 1906): 1.
50. A. H. Post, "Testimony of a Minister," *AF* (Los Angeles) (January 1907): 4.
51. Synan, *Holiness-Pentecostal Tradition*, 113.
52. James R. Goff, Jr., "The Pentecostal Catalyst To The South - G. B. Cashwell (1906-1909)", unpublished paper, 3.

was the fact of black leadership. He reached a crisis moment when a young black man approached him and inquired, "Do you want me to pray for you so that you will receive the Holy Ghost?"[54] According to Cashwell's testimony, that question caused "chills to go down my spine."[55] Yet the Holy Spirit communicated clearly to him that "this young man is deeply earnest, and I have sent him. How badly do you want to be filled?"[56]

Confronted with his racial prejudice, Cashwell, in classic Wesleyan fashion, had to lay it on the altar of sanctification if he hoped to receive the Spirit baptism. He reports that the next several days were spent dying to the old man. "As soon as I reached Azusa Mission, a new crucifiction [sic] began in my life and I had to die to many things, but God gave me the victory."[57] Each time he became aware of new sin in his life he wrote back to North Carolina asking for forgiveness.[58] Regarding the larger issue of his racial prejudice, Cashwell finally gave it up and on the fifth day asked Seymour and a few black elders to place hands upon him for the reception of Spirit baptism.[59] Cashwell's testimony recounts that in early December 1906, he received the baptism of the Holy Spirit and spoke in a "foreign" language.[60]

A short time later Cashwell was carrying the teaching of the three-stage experience to his home state and its surrounding neighbors. He exhorted them to get justified, receive sanctification, and then experience the baptism of the Holy Spirit with evidence of an unknown tongue.[61] In addition, after reporting the many things that God was doing among both whites and blacks during the revivals, he ended on the note that "all the people of God are one here."[62] Finally, in a stark turn around for a man who had earlier struggled with the role of black leadership, he now referred to Charles Mason, African-American leader of the interracial Church of God in Christ, as "a precious brother."[63]

His were not the only field reports verifying the role of sanctification in the formation of sanctified unity ecclesiology among racially and ethnically diverse believers. Thomas Hezmalhalch wrote to the saints in Los Angeles explaining the basis of the new-found unification of the body of Christ in

---

53. Synan, *Old-Time Power*, 73.

54. Carl Brumback, *Suddenly . . . from Heaven: A History of the Assemblies of God* (Springfield, Mo.: Gospel Publishing House, 1961), 84.

55. Synan, *Holiness-Pentecostal Tradition*, 113-114.

56. Brumback, *Suddenly . . . from Heaven*, 84.

57. G. B. Cashwell, "Came 3,000 Miles for His Pentecost," *AF* (Los Angeles) (December 1906): 3.

58. Goff, "Pentecostal Catalyst to the South", 3.

59. Synan, *Old-Time Power*, 107.

60. Goff, "Pentecostal Catalyst to the South", 3.

61. Cashwell, Gaston Barnabas, "Dunn, N.C.," *AF* (Los Angeles) (February-March 1907): 3.

62. G. B. Cashwell, "Pentecost in North Carolina," *AF* (Los Angeles) (January 1907): 1.

63. G. B. Cashwell, "In Memphis, Tenn., May 2," *AF* (Los Angeles) (May 1907): 1.

Needles, California. "There are thousands of Indians of different tribes in the mountains, and he meant they, and themselves, and the white people, and a colored brother, pointing to each of us, would, by the Blood of Jesus Christ, be made one great spiritual family."[64]

The prevalence of references to the spiritual leadership of non-Caucasians and the interracial and multiethnic unity of the faithful argues for the strong leadership of William Seymour. It was his vision more than anyone else's that drove early pentecostals to recognize that the bride of Christ is a diverse body and that the eschatological outpouring of the Spirit must result in sanctified unity communally, as well as corporately. Yet it cannot be missed that his years of ministry within radical holiness had shaped him both theologically and experientially to guide the nascent Pentecostal movement towards a theological position consistent with sanctified unity ecclesiology.

Spirit Baptism:
"Baptizing Them by One Spirit into One Body"

If the holiness doctrine of sanctification provided Seymour and the Azusa Street leadership the needed catalyst to practice sanctified unity ecclesiology, then the pentecostal power of Spirit Baptism completed the work. Interpreting Jesus' high priestly prayer through the lens of Galatians 3:28, *The Apostolic Faith* described the work of God thus: "This meeting has been a melting time. The people are all melted together by the power of the blood and the Holy Ghost. They are made one lump, one bread, all one body in Christ Jesus. There is no Jew or Gentile, bond or free, in the Azusa Street Mission."[65] At the start of the Azusa Street revival the leadership preached that the evidence of Spirit Baptism was speaking in a new tongue. Seymour had brought this doctrine with him from Houston, Texas, where he had sat under the teaching of Charles Parham. Seymour wrote in the first issue of *The Apostolic Faith* that the "Baptism with the Holy Ghost is a gift of power upon the sanctified life; so when we get it we have the same evidence as the Disciples received on the Day of Pentecost (Acts 2:3,4), in speaking in new tongues."[66] Spirit baptism confirmed the rightness of sanctified unity for the restored New Testament church since the Spirit only baptized those who were living in one accord, just as the first disciples were doing at Pentecost. As a result, the baptism of the Holy Spirit fulfilled the prophecy of Joel 2 that "in the last days, I will pour out of my Spirit on all flesh."

---

64. Thomas Hezmalhalch, "Among the Indians at Needles, California," *AF* (Los Angeles) (January 1907): 3.
65. *The Apostolic Faith* (Los Angeles) (December 1906): 1.
66. William J. Seymour, "The Precious Atonement," *AF* (Los Angeles) (September 1906): 2.

Additionally, the baptism of the Holy Spirit complemented the sanctified unity achieved through the blood of Jesus in sanctification. Here "all flesh" was interpreted broadly to include not only men and women, as the prophecy clearly states, but also all races. "He recognizes no flesh, no color, no names . . . God is uniting His people, baptizing them by one Spirit into one body."[67] Even more poignantly Seymour stated in an article, "Receive Ye the Holy Ghost," "But praise our God, He is now given and being poured out upon all flesh. All races, nations, and tongues are receiving the baptism with the Holy Ghost and fire, according to the prophecy of Joel."[68]

An unsigned and untitled article in the April, 1907 issue made it clear that the second and third members of the Trinity were working together to establish sanctified unity in the reconstituted Apostolic Faith,

> It is the Blood of Jesus that brings fellowship among the Christian family. The Blood of Jesus Christ is the strongest in the world. It makes all races and nations into one common family in the Lord and makes them all satisfied to be one. The Holy Ghost is the leader and He makes all one as Jesus prayed, "that they all may be one."[69]

For all the many pronouncements within *The Apostolic Faith*, it is clear that the Azusa Street community did not continue to meet the standard of sanctified unity fellowship set by the leadership in the early days of the revival. As Pentecostal historian Cecil Robeck has argued, a growing disenchantment developed, particularly in William Seymour, over the state of the eschatological community at the Apostolic Faith Mission.[70] As early as November 1906, Seymour warned against emphasizing speaking in tongues as the "Bible evidence" of Spirit baptism to the neglect of the purifying role of sanctification. "How watchful we must be to feed on the word and keep under the blood, or else we shall become sounding brass and tinkling cymbals."[71] By the middle of 1907 Seymour was at it again, chastising the faithful in *The Apostolic Faith* for their lack of brotherly love.

As the first pentecostals sought Spirit baptism they needed reminding that the result of the new Pentecost necessitated sanctified unity among the believers. Since the evidence of Spirit baptism was speaking in tongues, the Azusa Street participants apparently attached greater importance to this spiritual phenomenon than the creation of a new eschatological community. This ran counter to the original ecclesiological construction, which de-

---

67. "Beginning of a World Wide Revival," *The Apostolic Faith* (Los Angeles) (January 1907): 1.
68. William J. Seymour, "Receive Ye the Holy Ghost," *AF* (Los Angeles) (January 1907): 2.
69. *The Apostolic Faith* (Los Angeles) (April 1907): 3.
70. Robeck, "William J. Seymour," 87-88.
71. "Under the Blood," *The Apostolic Faith* (Los Angeles) (November 1906): 3. Even though this article is not signed by Seymour the language and phraseology is similar to his writing style.

manded the same unity as the original one hundred and twenty in the upper room prior to the reception of the baptism of the Holy Spirit. Accordingly, Seymour corrected the overemphasis placed on tongues and argued for the purity of the bride of Christ as the primary sign of Pentecost. "Tongues are one of the signs that go with every baptized person, but it is not the real evidence of the baptism in the everyday life. Your life must measure with the fruits of the Spirit. If you get angry, or speak evil, or backbite, I care not how many tongues you may have, you have not the baptism of the Holy Spirit."[72] As the issue remained unresolved, the leadership at the Apostolic Faith Mission expanded the number of "signs" that followed Spirit baptism to include a Wesleyan emphasis on holiness. At the end of 1907 and the beginning of 1908 they stated that both the "divine love" shown your brother and sister and the manifestation of tongues with signs following were "Bible evidence" of the baptism of the Holy Spirit.[73] It was stated again in *The Apostolic Faith*, "Tongues are not an evidence of salvation, but one of the signs that follow every Spirit-filled man and woman. . . ."[74] Finally, an unsigned piece in the May 1908 issue of the revival's periodical stated:

> The Pentecostal power, when you sum it all up, is just more of God's love. If it does not bring more love, it is simply a counterfeit. Pentecost means to live right in the 13th chapter of First Corinthians, which is the standard. When you live there, you have no trouble to keep salvation. This is Bible religion. It is not manufactured religion. Pentecost makes us love Jesus more and love our brothers more.[75]

So that the readership would not miss what the outcome of more love towards Jesus and our brothers meant, the writer of the article tacked on this final sentence: "It brings us all into one common family."[76]

Conclusion

To summarize, the leadership of the Azusa Street revival remained constant in their application of sanctified unity ecclesiology to the new eschatological outpouring that occurred in Los Angeles. The evidence, garnered from *The Apostolic Faith*, eyewitness accounts and early histories, convincingly demonstrates that radical holiness theology shaped the hermeneutical lens through which the revival was understood. The doctrines of healing, entire sanctification, premillennial dispensationalism and baptism of the Holy Spirit are all present at Azusa Street. The doctrine of sanctified unity

---

72. As quoted in Robeck, "William J. Seymour," 81.
73. *The Apostolic Faith* (Los Angeles) (October to January 1908): 2.
74. Ibid., 4.
75. *The Apostolic Faith* (Los Angeles) (May 1908): 3.
76. Ibid., 3.

should now be included on this list. Sanctified unity ecclesiology argued for the unity of the church, both corporately and communally. In radical holiness circles of the late nineteenth and early twentieth centuries the call for one church became quite pronounced, perhaps most notably expressed in John P. Brooks's book, *The Divine Church*. The ecclesiological development of communal unity, on the other hand, remained in primitive form until the Azusa Street revival.

It is here that William J. Seymour deserves great credit in bringing the doctrine and practice of the communal oneness of sanctified unity ecclesiology--that is, the practice of interracial and multiethnic fellowship--to the forefront of the revival. It is no accident that one of the hallmarks of the 1906 revival was its interracial fellowship. Seymour both nurtured it and advertised it. But if he worked out of a specific theological tradition, radical holiness, that provided a biblical foundation for racial and ethnic unity, he also innovated by drawing it into the first tier of major doctrines. This he accomplished through the integration of racial and ethnic unity into the major theological formulations that supported the ethos of the first pentecostals.

The unity of the body of Christ across racial, gender and class barriers runs like a line through the prevailing theological constructions of Azusa Street. Hence, Seymour contemplates the tie between eschatological restorationism, entire sanctification, the baptism of the Holy Spirit and worldwide evangelization, and the pertinence of sanctified unity ecclesiology. William Seymour believed that holiness was the key to restoring the apostolic community through the eschatological outpouring of the Holy Spirit. Consequently, every doctrine proffered at the Apostolic Faith Mission was ultimately at the service of holiness.

> There is no difference in quality between the baptism with the Holy Ghost and sanctification. They are both holiness. Sanctification is the Lord Jesus Christ crowned in your hearts and the baptism with the Holy Spirit is His power upon you. It is all holiness. It makes you more like Jesus. It is Jesus in justification, Jesus in sanctification and Jesus in the baptism with the Holy Ghost. If we follow Jesus, we will never have any other spirit but the Spirit of holiness....[77]

For Seymour this meant a return to the sanctified unity ecclesiology of the first century church. Under his leadership, the Azusa Street revival demonstrated that sanctified unity was possible, even if only for a short time. This was his great accomplishment.

---

77. "The Baptism with the Holy Ghost," *The Apostolic Faith* (Los Angeles) (October to January 1908): 4.

Conclusion

The practice of sanctified unity ecclesiology did not end with the Azusa Street revival. Radical holiness fellowships that accepted the pentecostal message, and those which did not, each continued to struggle over the next decade to sustain interracial and multiethnic congregations. In the end, however, it proved too much to maintain socially heterodox churches in the midst of an intensified policy of segregationism.

This fact of history should not diminish the great efforts and temporary success of black, brown and white saints to overcome racist attitudes and fellowship together at the turn of the twentieth century. It was a remarkable achievement in its own right and is made more remarkable still when the social structures then operating in American culture are considered. White racists used legal and illegal means to stamp the face of Jim Crow on American society. Intimidation came in multiple forms: economic, political, social and religious. As a result there was virtually no place in the land of segregationism for the races to meet on equal terms in America.

It was in the midst of this cultural nihilism that holiness radicals arrived to offer an alternative view of the church. Not interested in changing American society and yet unwilling to adhere to its segregationist dictates, the saints developed a theology of holiness that challenged the very foundation upon which American Jim Crow policies rested. Scientific and religious racism claimed that the separation of the races was in the very nature of things. It was this conception of "the very nature of things" which the adherents to radical holiness disputed. Or rather it was their belief in God's willingness to change a person's nature that caused them to postulate a different social arrangement, a new ecclesiology, for the varied ethnicities, races and nationalities living in the nation. The saints conceded that humanity in its present state of nature could not end the divisions that separated them. It is in a person's nature to sin and sin brings separation, first between God and humanity, and then between people. But what if the nature of a person could be altered or, more accurately, restored to its original state? They were not claiming something new, they contended, only calling for a return to the message of the New Testament, the biblical message of holiness and all that it meant for the church.

As direct descendents of the Holiness movement, holiness radicals retained the doctrine of entire sanctification as the centerpiece of their message. The doctrine of entire sanctification developed under the ministry and teaching of John Wesley. It was Wesley's conviction that the biblical conception of salvation was much more highly textured than taught by the Reformation fathers. In addition to the forgiveness that the believer experienced in justification, Wesley taught that the nature of a person must be made holy. Opposed to Luther's famous dictum that the Christian was simultaneously justified and still by nature a sinner, Wesley argued for a "full salvation" which transformed the believer into a justified saint.

As his message crossed the Atlantic and took root in American soil it was wedded to urban and frontier revivalism. The result was the birth of the Holiness movement where entire sanctification became the immediate goal of every seeker of holiness. The saints offered to the church a literal holiness, a "second blessing" that eradicated all vestiges of the sin nature. No longer bound to a carnal nature bent towards self-interest, the sanctified Christian could expect perfect love to guide her actions towards others. The radical implications of entire sanctification started to surface from within the Holiness movement in the last two decades of the nineteenth century.

The immediate implication of the "second blessing" was personal. Individuals praised the wondrous grace God gave in entire sanctification, grace to defeat sin and love your neighbor. The experience was overpowering and turned nominal, and even committed, Christians into powerful megaphones for the gospel of holiness. The sanctified believer, however, could not apprehend the many dimensions of Wesleyan holiness unless he lived it out among other people. This was the great social battlefield where holiness could be tested and sharpened. The saints knew that if they failed at loving their neighbors, or even enemies, then perfect love had not yet matured within their blood-washed hearts.

The call of Jesus on the lives of the saints to love those outside the church was one thing, but he also prayed for unity within the fellowship of the saints. In his high priestly prayer in John 17 Jesus stated clearly to his disciples that their unity would function as an apologetic for the faith. Since oneness of spirit and purpose was impossible for the self-centered man to achieve on his own, the world would recognize their unity as the work of God. Reading the entire prayer convinced radicals within the Holiness movement that the unity of the faithful must be predicated on their sanctification, since Jesus prayed for both holiness and unity for his followers. Thus the desire to see unity in the church was borne out of the Wesleyans' commitment to live out their holiness in the world, and was given warrant in Jesus' high priestly prayer. This discovery led the holiness radicals, beginning with Daniel Warner and the Church of God Reformation Movement, to call for a united church founded on holiness, or an ecclesiology of sanctified unity.

The first conclusion reached by holiness militants was that none of the existing denominational churches represented the church Jesus founded. Denominational churches, the saints argued, were inherently bent towards self-preservation and self-promotion. It was their lack of holiness, they reasoned, that kept them bound to their sectarian ways. This included the Methodist Episcopal Church, but more specifically the National Holiness Association. Although established to bring the holiness message to the churches, the latter had failed to grasp that true holiness leads to unity among Christians and does not cooperate with a denominational system. At issue in the critique of the holiness radicals was ecclesiology. The issue of ecclesiology drove a wedge between those who became holiness radicals and everyone else, including advocates of entire sanctification within the National Holiness Association. Holiness radicals contended that the New Testament application of sanctification extended beyond the individual to include the church. Simply put, there should be only one church.

As they searched the Scriptures for its rightful name, a consensus formed around the "Church of God" as the most common appellation of the New Testament church. Different eschatologies also developed to explain what had happened to the Church of God in its early history and to explain why it was being restored at this time. Nevertheless, when these ideas coalesced around an alternative conception of ecclesiology, a torrent of holiness folk fled the denominational confines of "Babylon" and took their rightful place in the Church of God.

The characteristics of the Church of God were holiness and unity, and one became a member when he or she entered into the Kingdom of God through the blood of Jesus. This meant that there were Christians still living in "Babylon" unaware that they belonged to the Church of God. As adherents to the Church of God concept stepped up their attacks on denominationalism, they worked hard to convince fellow believers to join them as part of the reestablished New Testament church. Those who did started a new chapter in American religious history.

Holiness radical ecclesiology, aided by its eschatology, served to undercut the legitimacy of every other traditional Christian church. It drew a line, placing every other Christian body on the opposite side, and defined itself as the one, holy, universal and apostolic church of the New Testament. Although it continued to share similar doctrinal positions on most issues with most denominations, it found it necessary to separate on the issue of ecclesiology.

What did the saints mean when they preached Christian unity? Their writings suggest that at first they thought little about unity in racial and ethnic terms. They concentrated their focus instead on the corporate nature of unity. The Church of God was a visible body of believers without any ecclesiastical division or segmentation. In the main, this was the central message of the radical Holiness movement. No one became a part of the Church of God until he or she took the decisive step to leave the denominational church.

What a surprise it was, then, when the saints discovered that their message of unity attracted whites, blacks, Hispanics, Native Americans, Asians and even Jews who sought to join the restored Church of God. Convinced that the corporate nature of the church should be one, they searched the Scriptures to discover a family portrait of the Church of God. While they accepted biblical arguments based on a theology of Creation–that all humanity had one father God and that they were made of the same blood–what really drew their attention was the New Testament supposition that in Christ there was no longer Jew or Gentile, but a new person. Thus, they discovered the communal concept of the Church of God in the writings of Paul. Paul provided the snapshot of the New Testament community. Out of the "neither Jew nor Gentile" passages emerged the interpretive key to explain the communal unity required in the Church of God. No longer were there two races, or for that matter a varied collection of ethnic groups, but a new humanity living in unity with all other new men and women. They were all made one in the blood of Jesus Christ. All vestiges of the old Adam, pride, racial prejudice and superiority, were cleansed away for good once the Christian placed all on the altar and died to himself, only to be reborn a sanctified man.

Sanctified unity ecclesiology clearly defined who was a part of the radical Holiness movement. Certainly there were men and women, such as Beverly Carradine, George Watson and Joanna P. Moore, who continued to operate on the boundary lines between radical holiness and mainstream holiness, and also kept their ties to mainline denominations. But the radical Holiness movement is best defined by those who crossed over from "Babylon" to the Church of God. And as sanctified Christians in the restored New Testament church, they were compelled by the teachings of Jesus and the writings of Paul to erase the color line within their own hearts and among the saints. There was "neither Jew nor Gentile" in the Church of God, but a new person in Christ Jesus.

The movement flourished among the saints and many pentecostals from 1880 into the early part of the twentieth century. It started in the flat lands of the Midwest and reached its apogee on the urban streets of Los Angeles. In between these dates and for a short time later, holiness radicals established sanctified unity fellowships all across the country in almost every region, including the South. Nevertheless, when segregationist policies and racial prejudice created an American apartheid, the nascent theology of sanctified unity ecclesiology could not withstand the pressure. But other factors also collaborated with the lack of a substantial theology to portend the end of interracial and multiethnic fellowships. For instance, the growing acceptance of premillennialism among the radical saints meant that all the energy of the movement became directed towards preparing people for the coming of Christ. Along with the constant legal and social obstacles placed in their path when attempting to rent space for their multiethnic revivals, the saints began to doubt the logic in continuing an ecclesiology that drove people away from their holiness message. Soon the holiness evangelists on the field were writing to their respective papers seeking advice on how to cut through this Gordian knot. When the two doctrines crossed paths on the mission field they created a theological tension for the militant saints, one which was not resolved until the "practical" solution of segregated revival services was adopted.

Additionally, holiness teaching increasingly became restricted to the personal realm–defined as a list of "do nots"–and vacated the social realm. Soon a saint's holiness was based on whether his apparel included or excluded a necktie, or depended on his diet. With the switch in emphasis from the social to the exclusively personal, and with the acceptance of premillennialism, the original desire to forge communal bonds across ethnic and racial lines came to an end. This is not too surprising, perhaps, when one considers that, with the exception of the Azusa Street revival, the conversation about the interracial and multiethnic communal aspects of sanctified unity ecclesiology always had played second chair to the corporate unity of the Church of God. Still, when the first and second chair played their music together, the world and the church seemed to witness the fulfillment of Jesus' last departing prayer request. When the first chair played solo the radical Holiness movement became just another divisive movement, once more rending the body of Christ and becoming a "sounding brass and a tinkling cymbal."

Bibliography

Primary Sources

Adams, Leonard P. File located at the Assemblies of God's Flower Pentecostal Heritage Center.

Bartleman, Frank. "How Pentecost Came to Los Angeles: As It Was in the Beginning." In *Witness to Pentecost: The Life of Frank Bartleman,* ed. Donald Dayton. New York: Garland, 1985.

Bartleman, Frank. "From Plow to Pulpit, from Maine to California." In *Witness to Pentecost: The Life of Frank Bartleman,* ed. Donald Dayton. New York: Garland, 1985.

Brooks, John P. *Divine Church.* New York: Garland, 1984 (first printing, 1891).

Carradine, Beverly. *The Sanctified Life.* Cincinnati, Ohio: M. W. Knapp, 1890.

Carroll, Chas. *The Negro a Beast or In the Image of God.* Miami, Fla: Mnemosyne, 1900.

Cobbins, Otho B., ed. *History of Church of Christ (Holiness) U.S.A 1895-1965.* New York: Vantage Press, 1966.

Courts, James, ed. *The History and Life Work of Elder C. H. Mason, Chief Apostle and His Co-Laborers.* N.p., 1920.

DuBois, W. E. B. *The Souls of Black Folk.* New York: Bantam Books, 1989.

Godbey, W. B. *Sanctification.* Dallas: Holiness Echoes, 1956 (first printing, 1884).

Hills, A. M. *The Cleansing Baptism.* Manchester: Star Hall, 1908.

Hills, Aaron Merritt. *A Hero of Faith and Prayer; or, Life of Rev. Martin Wells Knapp.* Cincinnati: Mrs. M.W. Knapp, 1902.

Juillerat, L. Howard. *Brief History of the Church of God.* Cleveland, Tenn.: Church of God Publishing House, 1922.

Knapp, Martin W. *Lightening Bolts from Pentecostal Skies, or Devices of the Devil Unmasked.* Jamestown, N.C.: Newby Book Room, n.d., originally 1898.

Knapp, Martin W. *Double Cure.* Cincinnati, Ohio: God's Revivalist Office, 1898.

Knapp, Martin W. *Christ Crowned Within.* Saratoga Springs, N.Y.: Marion Tract Depository, 1886.

Lawrence, Bennett F. *The Apostolic Faith Restored*. St. Louis, Mo.: Gospel, 1916 (reprint in the "Higher Christian Life" series, New York: Garland, 1985).

Mason, Mary [Esther], ed. *The History and Life Work of Elder C. H. Mason*. N.p., 1924.

Morris, Samuel. *Samuel Morris: A Spirit Filled Life*. Anderson, Ind.: Gospel Trumpet Company, 1908.

Myland, David W. *The Latter Rain Covenant*. Chicago: Evangel Publishing House, 1910.

Rees, Seth. *The Ideal Pentecostal Church*. Cincinnati, Ohio: M. W. Knapp, 1899.

Riggle, H. M. *The Christian Church: Its Rise and Progress*. Anderson, Ind.: Gospel Trumpet Company, 1912.

Schell, William G. *Is the Negro a Beast? A Reply to Charles Carroll's Book Entitled 'The Negro a Beast,' Proving That the Negro Is Human from Biblical, Scientific, and Historical Standpoint*. Moundsville, W.Va.: Gospel Trumpet Publ. Co., 1901.

Schell, William G. *The Better Testament; or, The Two Testaments Compared*. Moundsville, W.Va.: Gospel Trumpet Publishing Company, 1899.

Seymour, William J. *The Doctrines and Discipline of the Azusa Street Apostolic Faith Mission of Los Angeles, Cal., 1915*. Unpublished.

Smith, F. G. *What the Bible Teaches: A Systematic Presentation of the Fundamental Principles of Truth Contained in the Holy Scriptures*. Guthrie, Okla: Faith Publishing House, 1973.

Taylor, G. F. *The Spirit and the Bride*, in *Three Early Pentecostal Tracts*. Edited by Donald W. Dayton. New York: Garland, 1985.

Teel, George M. *The New Testament Church*. Los Angeles: Pentecost Printing House, 1901.

Warner, D. S. *Bible Proofs of the Second Work of Grace*. E.U.: Mennonite Publication Society, 1880.

Warner, D. S. *The Church of God, or What Is the Church and What Is Not*. Anderson, Ind: Gospel Trumpet Co., n.d.

Warner, D.S. and Riggle, H.M. *The Cleansing of the Sanctuary*. Moundsville, W. Va.: Gospel Trumpet Publishing Company, 1903.

Washburn, Josephine M. *History and Reminiscences of the Holiness Church Work in Southern California and Arizona*. New York: Garland, 1985.

Watson, George D. *Types of the Holy Spirit*. Dallas: Evangel, n.d..

Periodicals

Apostolic Faith (Los Angeles), 1906-1909.

Burning Bush, 1902, 1904

God's Revivalist and Bible Advocate (Cincinnati), 1901.

Gospel Trumpet (Indianapolis), 1881-1909.

Leaves of Healing (Chicago and Zion City, Illinois), 1899-1904.

Live Coals of Fire, 1899, 1900
Los Angeles Times, 1906, 1907.
Pentecost, 1886-1911
Revivalist (Cincinnati), 1888-1900.
Truth (Jackson, Mississippi), 1903.
Zion's Outlook (Nashville), 1901-1906.

Secondary Sources

Alexander, Estrelda Y. *Black Fire: One Hundred Years of African American Pentecostalism.* Downers Grove, IL.: IVP Academic, 2011.

Anderson, Robert Mapes. *Vision of the Disinherited: The Making of American Pentecostalism.* New York: Oxford University Press, 1979.

Bangs, Carl. *Phineas F. Bresee: His Life in Methodism, the Holiness Movement, and the Church of the Nazarene.* Kansas City, Mo.: Beacon Hill Press of Kansas City, 1995.

Beacham, Doug. *Azusa East: The Life and Times of G.B. Cashwell.* Franklin Springs, GA.: LSR Publications, 2006.

Benson, John T. *A History 1898-1915 of the Pentecostal Mission, Inc., Nashville, Tennessee.* Nashville, Tenn.: Trevecca Press, 1977.

Blumhofer, Edith. "Restoration as Revival: Early American Pentecostalism." In *Modern Christian Revivals*, ed. Edith Blumhofer and Randall Balmer. Urbana, Ill.: University of Illinois Press, 1993.

Blumhofer, Edith L. *Restoring the Faith: The Assemblies of God, Pentecostalism, and American Culture.* Urbana, Ill.: University of Illinois, 1993.

Brasher, J. Lawrence. *The Sanctified South: John Larkin Brasher and the Holiness Movement.* Urbana, Ill.: University of Illinois Press, 1994.

Brumback, Carl. *A Sound from Heaven.* Springfield, Mo.: Gospel Publishing House, 1977.

Brumback, Carl. *Suddenly . . . from Heaven: A History of the Assemblies of God.* Springfield, Mo.: Gospel Publishing House, 1961.

Burgess, Stanley M., and Gary B. McGee, eds. *Dictionary of Pentecostal and Charismatic Movements.* Grand Rapids: Zondervan, 1988.

Burgess, Stanley M., ed. *Reaching Beyond: Chapters in the History of Perfectionism.* Peabody, Mass.: Hendrickson, 1986.

Byers, A. L. *Birth of a Reformation: Or the Life and Labor of Daniel S. Warner.* Anderson, Ind.: Gospel Trumpet Company, 1921.

Callen, Barry L. "Daniel Sydney Warner: Joining Holiness and All Truth." *Wesleyan Theological Journal* 30 (Spring 1995): 92-110.

Callen, Barry L. *Contours of a Cause: The Theological Vision of the Church of God Movement (Anderson).* Anderson, Ind.: Old Paths Tract Society, 1995.

Callen, Barry L. *It's God's Church! The Life and Legacy of Daniel Sidney Warner.* Anderson, Ind.: Warner Press, 2002.

Campbell, Joseph E. *The Pentecostal Holiness Church 1898-1948.* Franklin Springs, Ga.: Publishing House of the Pentecostal Holiness Church, 1951.

Carter, Paul S. *Heritage of Holiness.* Self-Published, 1991.

Cerillo, Augustus, Jr. and Grant A. Wacker. "Bibliography and Historiography." In *The New International Dictionary of Pentecostal and Charismatic Movements,* ed. Stanley M. Burgess and Eduardo M. Van Der Maas, 382-405. Grand Rapids, Mich.: Zondervan, 2002.

Clear, Val. *Where the Saint Have Trod: A Social History of the Church of God Reformation Movement.* Chesterfield, Ind.: Midwest Publications, 1977.

Clemmons, Ithiel C. *Bishop C. H. Mason and the Roots of the Church of God in Christ.* Bakersfield, Calif.: Pneuma Life Publishing, 1996.

Clemmons, Ithiel C. *Profile of a Churchman, The Life of Otha M. Kelly in the Church of God in Christ.* Jamaica, N.Y.: K & C Publ., 1976.

Clemmons, Ithiel C. "True Koinonia: Pentecostal Hopes and Historical Realities." Paper presented at the 11th Annual Meeting of the Society for Pentecostal Studies, Charlotte, N.C., 1981.

Conn, Charles W. *Like a Mighty Army: A History of the Church of God, 1886-1976.* Cleveland, Tenn.: Pathway Press, 1975.

Cowen, Clarence E. *A History of the Church of God (Holiness).* Overland Park, Kans.: Herald and Banner Press, 1949.

Cox, Harvey. *Fire from Heaven: The Rise of Pentecostal Spirituality and the Reshaping of Religion in the Twenty-First Century.* Reading, Mass.: Addison-Wesley, 1995.

Creech, Joe. "Visions of Glory: The Place of the Azusa Street Revival in Pentecostal History." *Church History* 65 (Sept 1996): 405-424.

Crews, Mickey. *The Church of God: A Social History.* Knoxville, Tenn.: The University of Tennessee Press, 1990.

Cubie, David L. "A Wesleyan Perspective on Christian Unity." *Wesleyan Theological Journal* 33 (Fall 1998): 198-229.

Daniels, David D. "African-American Pentecostalism in the 20th Century." In *The Century of the Holy Spirit: 100 Years of Pentecostal and Charismatic Renewal, 1901-2001,* ed. Vinson Synan. Nashville, Tenn.: Thomas Nelson, 2001.

Daniels, David D. "Charles Harrison Mason: The Interracial Impulse of Early Pentecostalism." In *Portraits of a Generation: Early Pentecostal Leaders,* ed. James R. Goff, Jr. and Grant Wacker. Fayetteville, Ark.: The University of Arkansas Press, 2002.

Daniels, David D. "The Color of Charismatic Leadership: William Joseph Seymour and Martin Luther King, Jr. as Champions of Interracialism." In *We've Come This Far: Reflections on the Pentecostal Tradition and Racial Reconciliation,* ed. Byron D. Klaus. Springfield, MO.: Assemblies of God Theological Seminary, 2007.

Daniels, David D. "Navigating the Territory: Early Afro-Pentecostalism as a Movement within Black Civil Society." In *Afro-Pentecostalism: Black Pentecostal and Charismatic Christianity in History and Culture,* eds. Amos Yong and Estrelda Y. Alexander. New York and London: New York University Press, 2011.

Daniels, David D. "The Cultural Renewal of Slave Religion: Charles Price Jones and the Emergence of the Holiness Movement in Mississippi." Ph.D. diss., Union Theological Seminary, 1992.

Dann, Norman Kingsford. "Concurrent Social Movements: A Study of the Interrelationships between Populist Politics and Holiness Religion." Ph.D. diss., Syracuse University, 1974.

Dayton, Donald W. *Theological Roots of Pentecostalism.* Metuchen, N.J.: Scarecrow, 1987; reprint, Peabody, Mass.: Hendrickson, 1994.

Deno, Vivian Eilythia. "Holy Ghost Nation: Race, Gender, and Working-Class Pentecostalism, 1906-1926." Ph.D. diss., University of California, Irvine, 2002.

Dieter, Melvin E. *The Holiness Revival of the Nineteenth Century.* Lanham, Md.: Scarecrow Press, 1996.

Dieter, Melvin E. "Primitivism in the American Holiness Tradition." *Wesleyan Theological Journal* 30 (Spring, 1995): 78-91.

DuPree, Sherry S. "In the Sanctified Holiness Pentecostal Charismatic Movement." *Pneuma* 23 (Spring 2001): 97-114.

Espinosa, Gaston. "Borderland Religion: Los Angeles and the Origins of the Latino Pentecostal Movement in the U.S., Mexico, and Puerto Rico, 1900-1945." Ph.D. diss., University of California, Santa Barbara, 1999.

Faupel, D. William. *The Everlasting Gospel: The Significance of Eschatology in the Development of Pentecostal Thought.* Sheffield, England: Sheffield Academic Press, 1996.

Faupel, D. William. "William H. Durham and the Finished Work of Calvary." in *Pentecost, Mission and Ecumenism: Essays on Intercultural Theology,* ed. Jan A. B. Jongereel. Frankfurt and Main: Peter Lang, 1992.

Frodsham, Stanley H. *With Signs Following: The Story of the Pentecostal Revival in the Twentieth Century.* Springfield, Mo.: Gospel Publishing House, 1946.

Fudge, Thomas A. *Daniel Warner and the Paradox of Religious Democracy in Nineteenth-Century America.* Lewiston: E. Mellen Press, 1998.

Fulop, Timothy E. "'The Future Golden Day of the Race': Millennialism and Black Americans in the Nadir, 1877-1901." *Harvard Theological Review* 84 (1991): 75-99.

Goff, James R., Jr. *Fields White Unto Harvest: Charles F. Parham and the Missionary Origins of Pentecostalism.* Fayetteville, ArK: The University of Arkansas Press, 1988.

Goff, James R., Jr. "The Pentecostal Catalyst to the South - G. B. Cashwell (1906-1909)." Unpublished paper, 1980.

Goss, Ethel E. *The Winds of God: The Story of the Early Pentecostal Movement (1901-1914) In the Life of Howard A. Goss.* Hazelwood, Mo.: Word Aflame Press, 1958.

Haynes, Stephen R. *Noah's Curse: The Biblical Justification of American Slavery.* Oxford: Oxford University Press, 2002.

Hollenweger, Walter J. *Black Pentecostal Concept: Interpretation and Variations.* Geneva: World Council of Churches, 1970.

Hollenweger, Walter J. *Pentecostalism: Origins and Developments Worldwide.* Peabody, Mass.: Hendrickson, 1997.

Hughes, Richard T., ed. *The American Quest for the Primitive Church.* Urbana, Ill.: University of Illinois, 1988.

Hughes, Richard T., ed. *The Primitive Church in the Modern World.* Urbana, Ill.: University of Illinois, 1995.

Hughes, Richard T., and Leonard C. Allen, *Illusions of Innocence Protestant Primitives in America, 1630-1875.* Chicago, Ill.: University of Chicago Press, 1988.

Irvin, Dale T. "Charles Price Jones: Image of Holiness." In *Portraits of a Generation: Early Pentecostal Leaders,* ed. James R. Goff, Jr. and Grant Wacker. Fayetteville: The University of Arkansas Press, 2002.

Irvin, Dale T. "'Drawing All Together in One Bond of Love': The Ecumenical Vision of William J. Seymour and the Azusa Street Revival." *Journal of Pentecostal Theology,* no. 6 (April 1995): 25-33.

Jacobsen, Douglas. *Thinking in the Spirit: Theologies of the Early Pentecostal Movement.* Bloomington, Ind.: Indiana University Press, 2003.

Jones, Charles Edwin. "Beulah Land and the Upper Room: Reclaiming the Text in Turn-of-the-Century Holiness and Pentecostal Spirituality." *Methodist History* 32 (July 1994): 250-259.

Jones, Charles Edwin. "The 'Color Line' Washed Away in the Blood: In the Holiness Church at Azusa Street and Afterward." *Wesleyan Theological Journal* 34 (Fall, 1999): 252-265.

Jones, Charles Edwin. *A Guide to the Study of The Holiness Movement.* ATLA Bibliography Series, no. 1. Metuchen, N.J.: Scarecrow Press, 1974.

Jones, Charles Edwin. *A Guide to the Study of the Pentecostal Movement,* ATLA Bibliography Series, No. 6. Metuchen, N.J.,: Scarecrow Press, 1983.

Jones, Charles Edwin. *Perfectionist Persuasion: The Holiness Movement and American Methodism, 1867-1936.* Metuchen, N.J.: Scarecrow Press, 1974.

Jones, Kenneth. *Theology of Holiness and Love.* Lanham, Md.: University Press of America, 1995.

Kenyon, Howard N. "An Analysis of Ethical Issues in the History of The Assemblies of God." Ph.D. diss., Baylor University, 1988.

Kostlevy, William. "Nor Silver, Nor Gold: The Burning Bush Movement and the Communitarian Holiness Vision." Ph.D. diss., University of Notre Dame, 1996.

Lennox, John S. "Biblical Interpretation in the American Holiness Movement, 1875-1920." Ph.D. diss., Drew University, 1992.

Lewis, B. Scott, "William J. Seymour: Follower of the 'Evening Light'(Zech. 14:7)." *Wesleyan Theological Journal* 39, no. 2 (Fall, 2004): 167-183.

Lindstrom, Harald. *Wesley and Sanctification: A Study in the Doctrine of Salvation.* Nappanee, Ind.: Francis Asbury Press, 1980.

Litwack, Leon. *Trouble in Mind: Black Southerners in the Age of Jim Crow.* New York, N.Y.: Alfred A. Knopf, 1998.

Lovett, Leonard. "Black Holiness-Pentecostalism: Implications for Ethics and Social Transformation." Ph.D. diss., Emory University, 1978.

McClendon, James W. *Systematic Theology, vol.1, Ethics.* Nashville, Teen.: Abingdon, 1986.

McClurkan, James O. *Wholly Sanctified. What It Is and How It May Be Obtained.* Nashville, Tenn.: Self-Published, 1895.

McElhany, Gary D. "The South Aflame: A History of the Assemblies of God in the Gulf Region, 1901-1940." Ph.D. diss., Mississippi State University, 1996.

MacRoberts, Iain. *The Black Roots and White Racism of Early Pentecostalism in the USA.* London: MacMillan Press, 1988.

Martin, Larry, ed. *Holy Ghost Revival on Azusa Street: The True Believers.* Joplin, Mo.: Christian Life Books, 1998.

Massey, James Earl. *An Introduction to the Negro Churches in the Church of God Reformation Movement.* New York: Shining Light Survey Press, 1957.

Massey, James E. "Race Relations and the American Holiness Movement." *Wesleyan Theological Journal* 31 (Spring 1996): 40-50.

Massey, James Earl, and Thomas J. Sawyer. *Three Black Leaders of the Church of God Reformation Movement.* Anderson, Ind.: The Center for Pastoral Studies, Anderson School of Theology, 1981.

Mathews, Donald G. *Religion in the Old South.* Chicago: The University of Chicago Press, 1977.

Meier, August. *Negro Thought in America 1880-1915: Racial Ideologies in the Age Booker T. Washington.* Ann Arbor, Mich.: The University of Michigan Press, 1969.

Michel, David. *Telling the Story: Black Pentecostals in the Church of God.* Cleveland, Tenn.: Pathway Press, 2000.

Montgomery, William E. *Under Their Own Vine and Fig Tree: The African-American Church in the South 1865-1900.* Baton Rouge: Louisiana University Press, 1993.

Nelson, Douglas J. "For Such a Time as This: The Story of Bishop William J. Seymour and the Azusa Street Revival." Ph.D. diss., University of Birmingham, England, 1981.

Newman, Joe. *Race and the Assemblies of God Church: The Journey from Azusa Street to the "Miracle of Memphis."* Youngstown, New York: Cambria Press, 2007.

Paris, Peter J. *The Social Teaching of the Black Churches.* Philadelphia: Fortress, 1985.

Peters, John L. *Christian Perfection and American Methodism.* Grand Rapids, Mich.: Francis Asbury-Zondervan, 1985.

Reardon, Robert H. *The Early Morning Light.* Anderson, Ind.: Warner Press, 1979.

Reed, Rodney Layne. "Toward the Integrity of Social Ethics and Personal Ethics in the Holiness Movement, 1880-1910." Ph.D. diss., Drew University, 1995.

Reed, Rodney L. "Worship, Relevance, and the Preferential Option for the Poor in the Holiness Movement, 1880-1910." *Wesleyan Theological Journal* 32 (Fall 1997): 80-104.

Richardson, Harry V. *Dark Salvation: The Story of Methodism as It Developed among Blacks in America.* New York: Anchor/Doubleday, 1976.

Robeck, Cecil M., Jr. *The Azusa Street Mission & Revival: The Birth of the Global Pentecostal Movement.* Nashville, TN.: Thomas Nelson, Inc., 2006.

Robeck, Cecil M., Jr. "The Azusa Street Mission and Historic Black Churches: Two Worlds in Conflict in Los Angeles' African American Community." In *Afro-Pentecostalism: Black Pentecostal and Charismatic Christianity in History and Culture,* eds. Amos Yong and Estrelda Y. Alexander. New York and London: New York University Press, 2011.

Robeck, Cecil M., Jr. "Historical Roots of Racial Unity and Division in American Pentecostalism." Unpublished Paper.

Robeck, Cecil M., Jr. "William J. Seymour and 'The Bible Evidence.'" In *Initial Evidence: Historical and Biblical Perspectives on the Pentecostal Doctrine of Spirit Baptism,* ed. Gary B. McGee, 72-95. Peabody, Mass.: Hendrickson, 1991.

Robeck, Cecil M., Jr. "The Leadership Legacy of William J. Seymour." In *We've Come This Far: Reflections on the Pentecostal Tradition and Racial Reconciliation,* ed. Byron D. Klaus. Springfield, MO.: Assemblies of God Theological Seminary, 2007.

Robins, Roger G. *A. J. Tomlinson: Plainfolk Modernist.* Oxford: Oxford University Press, 2004.

Robins, Roger G. "A. J. Tomlinson: Plainfolk Modernist." In *Portraits of a Generation: Early Pentecostal Leaders,* ed. James R. Goff, Jr. and Grant A. Wacker. Fayetteville, Ark.: The University of Arkansas Press, 2002.

Robinson, Thomas A., "The Conservative Nature of Dissent in Early Pentecostalism: A Study of Charles F. Parham, the Founder of the Pentecostal Movement." In *Orthodoxy and Heresy in Religious Movements: Discipline and Dissent,* ed. Malcolm R. Greenshields and Thomas Robinson. Lewiston, N.Y.: Edwin Mellen, 1992.

Russell, Jean. *God's Lost Cause: A Study of the Church and the Racial Problem.* London: SCM, 1968.

Sanders, Cheryl J. "African-American Worship in the Pentecostal and Holiness Movements." *Wesleyan Theological Journal* 32 (Fall 1997): 105-120.

Sanders, Cheryl J. *Empowerment Ethics for a Liberated People: A Path to African American Social Transformation.* Minneapolis, Minn.: Fortress, 1995.

Sanders, Cheryl J. *Saints in Exile: The Holiness-Pentecostal Experience in African American Religion and Culture.* New York: Oxford University Press, 1996.

Sanders, Rufus Gene William. "The Life of William Joseph Seymour: Black Father of the Twentieth Century Pentecostal Movement." Ph.D. diss., Bowling Green State University, 2000.

Sernett, Milton C. *Black Religion and American Evangelicalism: White Protestants, Plantation Missions, and the Flowering of Negro Christianity, 1787-1865.* Metuchen, N.J.: Scarecrow Press, 1975.

Smith, H. Shelton. *In His Image, But...: Racism in Southern Religion, 1780-1910.* Durham, N.C.: Duke University Press, 1972.

Smith, John W. V. *Heralds of a Brighter Day: Biographical Sketches of Early Leaders in the Church of God Reformation Movement.* Anderson, Ind.: Gospel Trumpet Company, 1955.

Smith, John W. V. *The Quest for Holiness and Unity.* Anderson, Ind.: Warner Press, Inc., 1980.

Smith, Timothy L. *Called Unto Holiness: The Story of the Nazarenes.* Kansas City: Nazarene Publishing House, 1962.

Smith, Timothy L. "The Holiness Crusade." In *History of American Methodism*, ed. Emory S. Bucke, vol. 2. New York: Abingdon, 1964.

Stanley, John E. "Unity Amid Diversity: Interpreting the Book of Revelation In The Church of God (Anderson)." *Wesleyan Theological Journal* 25 (Fall 1990).

Stanley, Susie C. "Bumping into Modernity: Primitive/Modern Tensions in the Wesleyan/Holiness Movement." In *The Primitive Church in the Modern World*, ed. Richard T. Hughes. Urbana, Ill.: University of Illinois Press, 1995.

Strege, Merle D. *I Saw the Church: The Life of the Church of God Told Theologically.* Anderson, Ind.: Warner Press, 2002.

Strickland, William J., and H. Ray Dunning. *J. O. McClurkan: His Life, His Theology, and Selections from His Writings.* Nashville, Tenn., Trevecca Press, 1998.

Synan, Vinson. *The Old-Time Power.* Franklin Springs, Ga.: Advocate Press, 1973.

Synan, Vinson. *The Holiness-Pentecostal Tradition: Charismatic Movements in the Twentieth Century.* Grand Rapids, Mich.: Eerdmans, 1997.

Synan, Vinson & Charles R. Fox, Jr. *William J. Seymour: Pioneer of the Azusa Street Revival.* Alachua, FL.: Bridge-Logos, 2012.

Telfer, David A. *Red and Yellow, Black and White and Brown: Home Missions in the Church of God.* Anderson, Ind.: Warner Press, 1981.

Tinney, James S. "The Blackness of Pentecostalism." *Spirit: A Journal of Issues Incident to Black Pentecostalism* 3, No. 2 (1979): 27-35.

Tinney, James S. "Doctrinal Differences Between Black and White Pentecostals." *Spirit: A Journal of Issues Incident to Black Pentecostalism* 1, No. 1 (1977): 36-45.

Tinney, James S. "William J. Seymour: Father of Modern-Day Pentecostalism." In *Black Apostles*, ed. Randall K. Burkett and Richard Newman. Boston: G.K. Hall, 1978.

Wacker, Grant A. "Are the Golden Oldies Still Worth Playing? Reflection on History Writing among Early Pentecostals." *Pneuma* 8 (Fall 1986): 81-100.

Wacker, Grant A. "The Functions of Faith in Primitive Pentecostalism." *Harvard Theological Review* 77 (July/October 1984): 353-375.

Wacker, Grant A. *Heaven Below: Early Pentecostalism and American Culture.* Cambridge, Mass.: Harvard University Press, 2001.

Wacker, Grant A. "Playing for Keeps: The Primitivist Impulse in Early Pentecostalism." In *The American Quest for the Primitive* Church, ed. Richard T. Hughes, 196-219. Urbana, Ill.: University of Illinois, 1988.

Wacker, Grant A. "Searching for Eden with a Satellite Dish: Primitivism, Pragmatism, and the Pentecostal Character." In *The Primitive Church in the Modern World*, ed. Richard T. Hughes. Urbana, Ill.: University of Illinois Press, 1995.

Ware, Stephen J. "Restorationism in the Holiness Movement, Late Nineteenth and Early Twentieth Centuries." *Wesleyan Theological Journal* 34 (Spring 1999): 200-219.

Ware, Stephen J. "Restoring the New Testament Church: Varieties of Restoration in the Radical Holiness Movement of the Late Nineteenth and Early Twentieth Centuries." *Pneuma* 21 (Fall, 1999): 233-250.

Washington, James M. *Frustrated Fellowship: The Black Baptist Quest for Social Power.* Macon, Ga.: Mercer University Press, 1986.

Welch, Douglas E. "Jottings from the Archives." *Church of God Historian* 4, no. 1 (Fall 2003): 6-7.

Wheeler, Edward L. *Uplifting the Race: The Black Minister in the New South 1865-1902.* Lanham, Mass.: University Press of America, 1986.

White, Ronald C., Jr. *Liberty and Justice for All: Racial Reform and the Social Gospel (1877-1925).* San Francisco: Harper & Row, 1990.

Wills, David W. "The Central Themes of American Religious History: Pluralism, Puritanism, and the Encounter of Black and White." In *African-American Religion: Interpretive Essays in History and Culture*, ed. Timothy E. Fulop and Albert J. Raboteau, 9-20. New York: Routledge, 1997.

Woodward, C. Vann. *The Strange Career of Jim Crow.* New York: Oxford University Press, 1955.

Index

Lightning Source UK Ltd.
Milton Keynes UK
UKHW011835130522
402975UK00001B/82